SYLVIA de MARS
C LIN MURRAY
A TE O'DONOGHU
J WARWICK

D1344757

ORDERING TWO
NIONS

thern Ireland and Brexit

Leabharlanna Poibli Chathair Baile Átha Cliath

Dublin City Public Libraries

POLICY PRESS POLICY & PRACTICE

First published in Great Britain in 2018 by

Policy Press
University of Bristol
1-9 Old Park Hill
Bristol
BS2 8BB
UK
t: +44 (0)117 954 5940
pp-info@bristol.ac.uk
www.policypress.co.uk

North America office:
Policy Press
c/o The University of Chicago Press
1427 East 60th Street
Chicago, IL 60637, USA
t: +1 773 702 7700
f: +1 773 702 9756
sales@press.uchicago.edu
www.press.uchicago.edu

British Library Cataloguing in Publication Data
A catalogue record for this book is available from the British Library.

Library of Congress Cataloging-in-Publication Data
A catalog record for this book has been requested.

ISBN 978-1-4473-1724-1 (paperback)
ISBN 978-1-4473-4620-3 (ePub)
ISBN 978-1-4473-4621-0 (Mobi)
ISBN 978-1-4473-4622-7 (OA PDF)

The right of Sylvia de Mars, Colin Murray, Aoife O'Donoghue and Ben Warwick to be
identified as authors of this work has been asserted by them in accordance with the Copyright,
Designs and Patents Act 1988.

The statements and opinions contained within this publication are solely those of the authors
and not of the University of Bristol or Policy Press. The University of Bristol and Policy Press
disclaim responsibility for any injury to persons or property resulting from any material published
in this publication.

Policy Press works to counter discrimination on grounds of gender, race,
disability, age and sexuality.

Cover design by Policy Press
Front cover: image kindly supplied by Alamy
Printed and bound in Great Britain by CMP, Poole
Policy Press uses environmentally responsible print partners

Contents

Acknowledgements

We gratefully acknowledge the financial support of the UK's Economic and Social Research Council (grant ref. ES/M500513/1), which made this book possible. Our three universities – Birmingham, Durham and Newcastle – have supported us in various ways in the process of writing this book and in the years of research prior to it. We owe much to the many colleagues in our own universities and elsewhere who have been sounding boards, sources of inspiration and moral supporters.

We have enjoyed the input of more people than could be mentioned here, but we are especially appreciative of thought-provoking questions and comments we received from Kevin Brown, John Curtis, Elektra Garvie-Adams, Katy Hayward, Holger Hestermeyer, Paula Kelly, Daithí Mac Síthigh, Roger Masterman, Claire McCann and Sam Owen. We would also like to thank staff at Warwick Law School, the International Boundaries Research Unit at Durham University, the Transitional Justice Institute at Ulster University and Oxford's Programme for the Foundations of Law and Constitutional Government for letting us test some of the ideas in this book at staff seminars. We were also fortunate to receive detailed comments from our anonymous reviewers.

We very much appreciate the research assistance provided by Sumaiyah Kholwadia, Sarah Jane Price and Sophie Doherty, the assistance of Tina Martin in preparing the manuscript, and all the team at Policy Press (especially Helen Davis and

Rebecca Tomlinson) for their work on the project. On Twitter, @gavmacn put us on to our cover image; a gate without a fence is fast becoming a pretty good metaphor for some of the more bizarre attempts to find a solution to the conundrum that the Irish border poses for Brexit.

Finally, our thanks are due to our (long-suffering) families and friends, who, by now, understand too much about customs unions and categories of rights holder. Their support and understanding kept us going, particularly at those crunch moments when we did not have a lot of support for each other to spare.

In the fast-moving context of Brexit, we have sought to bring our account up to date as of 1 June 2018, but have been able to incorporate some further updates thanks to the efforts of the Policy Press team.

Sylvia, Colin, Aoife and Ben
June 2018

Glossary

Charter of Fundamental Rights (CFR): The EU's human rights document. All EU law must meet its standards and those standards are significant, going beyond what otherwise exists in UK law.

Common Travel Area: An umbrella term for a scattering of understandings and reciprocal agreements between the UK and Ireland (and surrounding islands) regarding rights and respect for each other's citizens.

Customs union: When countries in an FTA agree to apply a single customs policy to outsider (or 'third') countries at their external borders.

Dáil: This is the name for the directly elected lower house of the Irish Parliament/Oireachtas.

European Union (Withdrawal) Act 2018: The first major piece of law to make its way through the UK Parliament to facilitate Brexit. Parliamentarians have made and attempted many amendments to it. At the time of writing, it has not been concluded as law.

Free trade agreement (FTA): An agreement between two or more countries not to apply customs charges to (certain) goods at their shared border.

Garda: An Garda Síochána is the official name of the Irish police force.

Good Friday Agreement (GFA): Formally known as the Belfast Agreement, this is the 1998 peace agreement for

Northern Ireland, approved by referenda North and South of the border.

Irish Free State/Ireland/Republic of Ireland: On independence in 1922, Ireland was known as the Irish Free State/Saorstát Éireann. On the passing of the 1937 Constitution, the state became known as Ireland/Éire. Republic of Ireland is a description of Ireland that came out of the Republic of Ireland Act 1949; however, it is not the official name of the state.

Joint Report: The agreement between the UK and EU in December 2017 that marked 'significant progress' on major negotiating issues.

Oireachtas: This is the collective name for the joint houses of the Irish Parliament, the Dáil and the Seanad.

Protocol on Ireland/Northern Ireland: An annex to the Withdrawal Agreement specifically addressing the island of Ireland. It is not yet binding, but has substantial agreement in principle or on an exact form of proposed text.

Seanad: This is the name for the largely indirectly elected upper house of the Irish Parliament/Oireachtas.

Single market: A further agreement between the countries in an FTA or a customs union that goes beyond customs matters and, instead, focuses on the development of shared regulations, standards and institutions. (The European Union [EU] Single Market is also regularly called the 'Common Market' or the 'Internal Market'.)

Stormont: A name used as shorthand for the Northern Ireland Assembly (since 1998) and for the earlier Northern Ireland Parliament (1921–72).

Tánaiste: The title of the Irish Deputy Prime Minister.

Taoiseach: The title of the Irish Prime Minister.

Withdrawal Agreement: The draft legal text produced by the EU to transpose the Joint Report into legal provisions. It is currently not concluded or fully agreed, and either the UK or EU could still walk away from it to cause a 'no-deal' Brexit.

Abbreviations

CFR	European Union Charter of Fundamental Rights
CJEU	Court of Justice of the European Union
DExEU	Department for Exiting the European Union
DUP	Democratic Unionist Party
EAW	European Arrest Warrant
ECHR	European Convention on Human Rights
EEC	European Economic Community
EU	European Union
FTA	Free trade agreement
GFA	Good Friday/Belfast Agreement
IHREC	Irish Human Rights and Equality Commission
NIA	Northern Ireland Act 1998
NIAC	House of Commons Northern Ireland Affairs Committee
NIHRC	Northern Ireland Human Rights Commission
PSNI	Police Service of Northern Ireland
SPS	Sanitary and phytosanitary
UK	United Kingdom
WTO	World Trade Organization

ONE

A tale of two unions

'We do not wish … [the referendum] to be used for their own purposes by those who wish to divide the United Kingdom.' He [Edward Short, MP] went on to say, 'We are not concerned with what Northern Ireland thinks,' in words hardly felicitous for the occasion. (John Peyton, MP, 1975)

The people have spoken

As the referendum results edged towards a conclusion on that fateful June night, Northern Ireland was, as expected, an outlier. Many Unionist MPs had castigated the European project ahead of the vote, whereas Nationalist politicians had tended to emphasise its benefits in diminishing the significance of the Irish border. The Democratic Unionist Party's (DUP's) Ian Paisley had thundered through the campaign about the perils of 'a Roman Catholic super-state' that should be 'totally repugnant to freedom-loving Protestants'. When the tallies were finalised, a 52%/48% split loomed large, but Northern Ireland had voted in favour of membership.

That referendum, however, was in June 1975, not June 2016. Then, Northern Ireland had been considerably less enthusiastic about the European project than the remainder of the UK. Its 52% 'yes' vote contrasted with overall UK electorate support for membership of the-then European Economic Community of 67% (Dixon, 1994, pp 177–8). Whereas many Unionist politicians remained concerned over the dilution of UK sovereignty inherent in European membership, most Northern Ireland voters were swayed by more day-to-day concerns. Fast-forward to 2016 and Northern Ireland was one of the most pro-European parts of the UK. While the preceding quotes come from Ian Paisley Sr (Royce, 2017), in 2016, his son and namesake, who vigorously supported Brexit, happily declared his willingness to sign Irish passport forms for any of his constituents eager to maintain their European Union (EU) citizenship (Peyton, 2016).

Since the June 2016 vote, much of political life in Northern Ireland has focused upon the implications of Brexit. This book is about Northern Ireland's relationships with two unions (the UK and the EU), how those relationships have changed over the last few decades and how they will change again when the UK leaves the EU. We also consider how Ireland and its relationship with the EU continues to be influenced by developments in Northern Ireland.

The United Kingdom(s)

Northern Ireland's place within the first union featured in this book – the UK – has been fraught from its creation in 1921. In the early 20th century, 'centrifugal' (pushing away from the centre) and 'centripetal' (pulling towards the centre) forces destabilised the union that had existed between Ireland and Great Britain since 1801, requiring the creation of two new constitutional settlements on the island of Ireland (Calvert, 1968, p 3). At least, that is one way of explaining Irish history. The use of such abstract terms to characterise the partition of Ireland in the early 1920s should, however, come with a health warning. Sterile legal writing often disguises the intense human suffering produced when, within a restricted geographical space, two communities divided by faith, ethnicity and nationalism each attempt to impose their preferred vision for society on the other.

Partition broke, and simultaneously reinvented, the UK. The centrifugal force of Irish Nationalism spun the Irish Free State out of Westminster's orbit, taking much of the island of Ireland out of the Union. The United Kingdom of Great Britain and Ireland transformed into the United Kingdom of Great Britain and Northern Ireland. Unionism, which increasingly became a brand of 'Ulster nationalism', acted as a centripetal force keeping the six counties of the province of Ulster that made up Northern Ireland within the Union. Even with its place in the UK secured, Northern Ireland took shape as a territory at the constitutional margins – part of the Union, but with autonomous institutions based at Stormont, near Belfast.

Partition of the island of Ireland and devolution for Northern Ireland as a 'solution' to the Irish Question (Taylor, 1971) proved to be as unstable as the Union of Britain and Ireland that preceded it. It left a large community of Irish Nationalists within Northern Ireland. Their political ambitions unfulfilled, Nationalists were viewed by much of the larger Unionist community as being intent upon undermining the Union with Britain. In the late 1960s, decades of prejudice and suspicion boiled over into the Northern Ireland conflict. The first era of devolution in Northern Ireland ended ignominiously in March 1972 with the collapse of the Stormont Assembly amid a seemingly inexorable slide into civil war. For the next three decades, life in Northern Ireland would be characterised by conflict.

Then came the Good Friday/Belfast Agreement of 1998 (GFA), supported by over 71% of the Northern Ireland electorate in a subsequent referendum. Political violence within Northern

Ireland has declined dramatically following this deal, but peace has not necessarily brought with it the system of governance that was promised. The GFA mandated the creation of devolved institutions that operated on a power-sharing model, obliging parties from across the divide in Northern Ireland to cooperate in governance and law-making (GFA, Strand 1). Power sharing within Northern Ireland was supported by North–South cooperation (between Northern Ireland and the Republic of Ireland) (GFA, Strand 2) and East–West cooperation (between the Republic of Ireland and the UK as a whole) (GFA, Strand 3). The GFA would be augmented and amended by a series of agreements, from St Andrews in 2006 to Fresh Start in 2015, each one an effort to sustain power sharing and to paper over various breakdowns and crises. Although several elements of the GFA framework remain unfulfilled, including the promise of a Northern Ireland Bill of Rights, there have been significant successes, including the expansion of cross-border trade and cooperation on energy, tourism and health care across the island.

The unnaturalness of the GFA's neat division of Northern Ireland's people into Unionists and Nationalists (as well as a far less defined category of 'others') is inescapable. The division is a legacy of the conflict that the deal halted, but one that is increasingly divorced from the realities of 21st-century Northern Ireland. Using census data as a rough proxy, today, some 65% of the population identify as British (Unionist) or Irish (Nationalist), with a sizable portion instead seeing themselves as Northern Irish (21%) or as having hybrid British–Irish–Northern Irish identities (9%), or as not identifying as British, Irish or Northern Irish (5%) (Northern Ireland Statistics and Research Agency, 2012, p 15). This complexity is often poorly served by with a political culture in which diverse voices are often ignored or drowned out.

The European Union

Nearly two decades of on-and-off cooperation abruptly lurched to a standstill in January 2017. The immediate pretext for the collapse of the power-sharing Executive, and the inability to form another after the subsequent Assembly elections, was a clash between the main Nationalist party (Sinn Féin) and the main Unionist party (the DUP) over the waste and possible misuse of public funds through the Renewable Heating Incentive Scheme. However, it is Northern Ireland's place in the other union in our story – the EU – that has exacerbated the rift between these parties.

EU membership has changed the dynamic of relations between the UK and Ireland. In the 1960s, when the UK was Ireland's biggest market, Ireland was all but obliged to follow the UK's efforts to join the European project. However, for Ireland, it was vital that when both it and the UK joined in 1973, they did so as equal members (Arthur, 2000, p 129). From this basis of mutual respect, the representatives of these English-speaking islands on Europe's north-west periphery found that they shared many common policy interests. European summits obliged ministers from both countries to participate in the collegial 'family photographs' and enabled them to forge 'quiet cooperation' in a context less burdened with expectation than the intermittent bilateral meetings that had characterised the dark days of the early 1970s (Hainsworth, 1981, p 7).

Today, the EU's role in Northern Ireland life is so pervasive that it frequently goes unnoticed. Nonetheless, its farm payments under the Common Agricultural Policy and development funding have a bigger impact on the Northern Ireland economy than on any other part of the UK. Its combination of Northern Ireland and Ireland into a single agricultural regulating area was vital during events such as the Foot and Mouth crisis in 2001. The single market provided the opportunity for cross-border business to flourish, and the EU directly supported the peace process through tranches of PEACE Programme funding (Murphy, 2016, pp 142–8).

Brexit upends this picture, beginning with the undermining of the uneasy partnership between Sinn Féin and the DUP in the 2016–17 Executive. They campaigned on opposite sides of the 2016 referendum. In removing the commonalities between Ireland and the UK provided by the EU framework, Sinn Féin regarded Brexit as tilting Northern Ireland's constitutional balance towards London and away from Dublin. Post-Brexit, the DUP likewise became increasingly distrustful of Sinn Féin, which it saw as using Brexit to agitate for a border poll in Northern Ireland. Brexit, moreover, tore a hole in the 2016–17 Executive's programme for government. The potential transfer of competence for corporation tax to Northern Ireland under the Corporation Tax (Northern Ireland) Act 2015 provided the basis for the Executive's flagship economic policy. By lowering corporation tax to 12.5% to make Northern Ireland more competitive with the Republic of Ireland, the Executive hoped to have greater success in attracting inward investment. The uncertainty surrounding Brexit, however, undermined such opportunities.

In short, Northern Ireland is one of the most challenging aspects of Brexit because its relationship with both the UK and EU is so distinctive. Societal attitudes towards these two unions have been shaped by different concerns from those at work in Scotland, Wales and England, and Brexit will once again reshape these relationships. Key issues in the Brexit negotiations, such as the control of borders, citizenship rights, freedom of movement and access to foreign markets, have distinct resonances and impacts within Northern Ireland. Moreover, Strands 2 and 3 of the GFA, which managed to run on autopilot during every interminable power-sharing crisis in Northern Ireland, stand to be hollowed out when the UK leaves the common frameworks of the EU.

Most dangerously of all, however, Brexit stands to create winners and losers within Northern Ireland. Any changes in Northern Ireland's constitutional status that tie it closer into Westminster's orbit seem to affirm a Unionist vision of Northern Ireland's place in the world. On the other hand, any recognition in the Brexit deal of a special place for Northern Ireland under aspects of EU law could be interpreted as having the opposite effect of bringing it into closer alignment with Dublin. No shared approach to governance can easily sustain winners and losers on such key issues.

The shape of things to come

In this book, we unpack the significance of Brexit for the future of Northern Ireland by examining how Northern Ireland has shaped (and continues to shape) some of the most important struggles within the UK–EU withdrawal negotiations. This book is intended for anyone interested in how Brexit will change Northern Ireland, and how Northern Ireland is changing Brexit (for the UK as a whole, for Ireland and for the wider EU). We seek to shed some light on a series of fraught issues: what role EU membership plays in the Northern Ireland peace process; how Brexit could change identity in Northern Ireland; what Brexit means for different groups in Northern Ireland's society; whether Brexit can be compatible with the GFA; and how Brexit could alter our understanding of Northern Ireland's place within the UK and its constitutional relationship with Ireland. All of those questions carry with them a weight of technical legal terminology. If the Brexit debate seems shrouded in mysteries, like the difference between a single market and a customs union, what it means to claim EU citizenship, and the nature of maximum facilitation and regulatory alignment, we will try to explain the impact of these concepts in the Northern Ireland context.

No small volume like this one could hope to comprehensively cover the Northern Ireland aspects of Brexit; instead, we address one pressing issue in each of the following chapters. We start by examining the nature of the Irish border, from its creation to the radical changes of the late 20th century, and of the influence of the UK's and Ireland's EU membership upon that border. We then examine aspects of Brexit in turn, with chapters tackling how Northern Ireland became such a major feature in the Brexit negotiations on trade, citizenship, human rights and justice. Having sketched how Brexit will affect Northern Ireland, we come to evaluate the profound implications for the constitutions of Ireland and the UK as a whole of the emerging settlement for this one small part of the UK. We close by considering the cumulative impact of what has already been agreed within these areas of negotiation for Northern Ireland's status as part of the UK in a special relationship with the EU.

It is impossible to write about Brexit's impact upon Northern Ireland without using disputed language. Many Nationalists continue to refer to Northern Ireland as 'the North', demonstrating their opposition to the partition of Ireland (Sales, 1997, pp 3–4). However, as the GFA repeatedly uses the term 'Northern Ireland' and it has therefore received the endorsement of the people of Northern Ireland in the GFA referendum in 1998, we try to stick to that term.[1] The name for the Agreement itself remains something of a fraught issue, with some Unionists avoiding the use of the term 'Good Friday Agreement' because of its religious overtones and supposed links to the Easter Rising (Morgan, 2011, pp 3–4). However, the deal was widely referred to by Unionist politicians as the 'Good Friday Agreement' in the late 1990s before these suspicions developed. Rather than an inelegant compound term, we use the acronym 'GFA'

---

[1] Admittedly, the GFA also repeatedly uses 'North and South' as shorthand, so we will not feel so constrained as to plod through 'Northern Ireland and Ireland' at every time of asking.

throughout. Nationalists, Unionists and Republicans are all treated as proper nouns in our work. While the terms used and analysis provided in the following pages are unlikely to satisfy everyone, we have set out to be even-handed in our treatment of sincerely held positions.

TWO

Navigating the Irish border

[I]t is better that we should not even mention Partition in international assemblies, for our doing so would savour of the old coercionist policy of enlisting outside support against our fellow-countrymen, and, like that policy, would merely irritate without effecting any useful purpose. (Donal Barrington, 1957, p 400)

Introduction

Discussion of the challenges that the Irish border poses for Brexit has tended to quite literally size up the problem; the border, we are solemnly informed, is 310 miles in length, features over 200 formal crossings and is traversed by some 30,000 people daily for purposes of work alone (NIAC, 2018a, paras 5–7). Such approaches give the image of borders as narrow spaces at which checks on travellers and goods can occur, and the risk of a 'hardening' of the border between Northern Ireland and Ireland on Brexit comes to be seen solely in terms of extra checks and delays. Borders, however, also operate on a deeper level; partition in Ireland created separate political and legal orders where no formal divisions had existed before. When the European Union (EU) has done so much to standardise rules and regulations applicable on either side of the Irish border, any 'hardening' of this dividing line could produce increasingly pronounced divergences.

In this book, we approach the Irish land border as *both* a narrow space at which regulation happens (which could become much more highly regulated post-Brexit) and a deeper divide between two states (which could pursue increasingly divergent policies post-Brexit). Before we do that, however, we outline the legal topography of the border: the major concepts and laws that shape our understanding of this divide. We do not follow a fixed timeline of legislation because, over the last century, some aspects of the border were being hardened at the same time as others were being softened. Instead, we first explain the legal divisions erected with partition (the division of the island into the Irish Free State and Northern Ireland) and their impacts on Northern Ireland and the Republic of Ireland (the '*bordering*' of Ireland). We then identify the various ways in which law and politics have softened the border over time (the substantial '*de-bordering*' of Ireland). Finally, we will highlight the key stages in the Brexit process to date (leading to the potential '*re-bordering*' of Ireland).

Bordering

Partition

Talk of 800 years of British rule in Ireland creates an inaccurate image of continuous close control. At the end of the 18th century, the Irish Sea remained a distinct legal border. Ireland might have been a UK colony, but the UK Prime Minister Pitt the Younger had been unable to secure the Irish Parliament's consent to a free trade agreement between Britain and Ireland in the 1780s (Schweitzer, 1984, pp 129–30). Only with a rebellion in Ireland in 1798 and the threat of French invasion did things change; the Act of Union incorporated Ireland not only into the direct reach of Westminster, but also into a customs union with Britain (*Act of Union 1800*, Article VI). The Irish War of Independence ended with the creation of the Irish Free State and Northern Ireland as two separate jurisdictions through what became known as 'partition'. The rules on the customs union between Ireland and Britain no longer applied to the new Irish Free State. The fracturing of the Union was nonetheless partial; the violent separatism of the Easter Rising and the War of Independence of 1919–21 ended hopes not only that most Nationalists would accept limited autonomy within the UK (Foster, 2007, p 145), but also that most Northern Unionists would be reconciled to devolution for Ireland as a whole within the UK ('Home Rule'). Ireland was divided.

Between the 1920s and 1970s, partition became the defining aspect of the UK's relations with Ireland, with the land border providing a focal point. Once the Boundary Commission's efforts to adjust the border line came to nothing in the mid-1920s, approved routes were designated for the cross-border transit of goods and customs posts were established. As we will discuss further in Chapter Three, this caused serious dislocations of border life: train lines that criss-crossed the border soon closed; small businesses in border counties lost access to their suppliers or markets; and diverging laws on either side of the border encouraged the smuggling of everything from white bread to condoms. On a deeper level, the 'authoritarian and homogenizing instincts' of governments in both parts of the island of Ireland meant that the border became a means of looking inward in an effort to control their own populations (Leary, 2016, p 124). Until the late 1960s the government in London largely left the Stormont government in Northern Ireland to its own devices.

The early years of partition were marked by a Free State boycott of goods from Northern Ireland, officially as a protest against ongoing sectarian violence against its Nationalist minority but viewed by Unionists as a naked attempt at industrial protectionism (Good, 1922, pp 270–1). These changes in Ireland were capped by Articles 2 and 3 of the 1937 Irish Constitution, which made territorial claims over the entire island and thereby denied the legitimacy of Northern Ireland. In 1956, the Northern Ireland government published *Why the Border Must Be*, a staunch defence of partition, in which Ireland was crudely caricatured as a backwards-looking place of censorship and poverty (Northern Ireland Government, 1956). Its target was not the people of Northern Ireland, but only its own supporters. The border had become a mirror, reflecting back the image that ministers North and South wanted their own people to see and distracting them from internal woes.

Conflict

Although centuries of UK government policy had fostered divisions in Ireland, the border became 'an external symptom of an internal disease' (Horgan, 1939, p 425). Partition reflected intractable identity divisions. However, the border also left a sizable minority of Nationalists in Northern Ireland cut off from their majority on the island as a whole. Decades went by without high-level official contacts between the governments on either side of the border, and when Taoiseach Seán Lemass and Northern Ireland's Prime Minister Terence O'Neill did meet in 1965, the moment was fleeting and the discussions were insubstantial (Patterson, 1999, p 146). Instead, given the intense politicisation of the land border, it quickly became a focal point for political violence. Attacks on border posts in the 1920s, 1930s and 1950s were part of an undercurrent of political violence in Northern Ireland that while not as intense as during the later conflict, was nonetheless considerable. The 1960s saw political inertia gradually give way to tension; impatience within Nationalism about discrimination spurred on the Northern Ireland Civil Rights Movement, while increasing concerns among Unionist politicians over Northern Ireland's changing demography (two thirds of Northern Ireland's population identified as Protestant in 1926, but under half by 2001) stoked a backlash. As the conflict intensified and the UK armed forces were deployed in 1969, the border became intensely militarised, and the border counties became 'bandit country'. The division of Ireland became ringed with barbed wire and cast in concrete.

De-bordering

The Common Travel Area

Since the foundation of the Irish Free State, the position of Irish citizens in the UK and of UK citizens in Ireland has been unique: both countries treat each other's nationals as equivalent to citizens in most respects. The openness of travel between the two countries dates from 1922, when the Irish Free State decided to enforce the same travel arrangements as those in place in the UK. Neither country required passports for cross-border travel, a 'pragmatic' response to the difficulties in establishing 'an effective immigration frontier at the Irish border' (Ryan, 2001, p 874). Following the declaration making Ireland a Republic in 1949, UK legislation formalised this special relationship by declaring that Ireland, while no longer part of the UK, nor a dominion of the UK, nor even part of the Commonwealth, would not be treated in law as a 'foreign country', with all of the implications that would have for immigration law (*Ireland Act 1949 (UK)*, section 2).

In 1952, a new administrative agreement was reached, 'formalising' the Common Travel Area. This travel area covers both states, the Channel Islands and the Isle of Man. It enables UK and Irish nationals to be treated almost identically within both states. For example, UK citizens in Ireland and Irish citizens in the UK have the right to vote in local, national and European elections. Both sets of migrants enjoy access to employment, social welfare and health care on the same basis as citizens; they are not treated as 'aliens'. The few exceptions to this equal treatment are political in nature: although Irish citizens can run for the UK Parliament, non-Irish citizens cannot be elected to the Dáil, nor can they vote in constitutional referendums or presidential elections. The Common Travel Area helped to characterise a border between the two nations that was 'highly permeable' to people and ideas (Chubb, 1986, p 22), with the irony that with the strife of the 1970s to 1990s, the sea border between Great Britain and Ireland was easier to traverse than the increasingly militarised land border with Northern Ireland.

The GFA

The GFA marked just one step in the Northern Ireland peace process and much had happened before 1998. In the early 1970s, academics could confidently state that the UK's sovereignty over Northern Ireland was 'full and complete' (Beckett, 1971, p 126). After the Anglo-Irish Agreement of 1985 and the Downing Street Declaration of 1993, however, Ireland had attained 'a central role in any constitutional developments regarding Northern Ireland' (Morrison and Livingstone, 1995, p 148).

The meaning of some of the main GFA terms, especially North–South cooperation, choice of identity, cross-border equivalence of rights and the principle of consent, will be spelled out in the following chapters. However, much of this ground is disputed territory. Within the space of a week in April 2018, David Trimble characterised Brexit as all but irrelevant for the GFA, and presented the EU's draft withdrawal agreement as a threat to the GFA's underlying principles (Clarke, 2018; McDonald, 2018). These positions should be mutually incompatible, and perhaps with regard to any other polity, they would be. Instead, they illustrate a key aspect of post-GFA governance in Northern Ireland: either everyone must be seen to be winning, or no one must be seen to be winning. If constitutional upheavals affecting the 1998 peace settlement are not packaged in respectable deceptions or constructive ambiguities, they will not work.

The EU

The GFA includes little direct mention of the EU; for the UK Supreme Court, the GFA 'assumed' but did not 'require' the UK's continuing membership of the EU.[1] The assumption was nonetheless particularly important for many actors in the peace process. Ireland and the UK both working together as EU member states and passing over areas of legislative competence to EU institutions diluted the clash of nationalisms at work within Northern Ireland's society (Ritchie, 2017). Moreover, with the 'completion' of the EU's Single Market in 1993, physical manifestations of the border, such as the customs posts at Newry and Dundalk, were closed. Once the security architecture linked to the Northern Ireland conflict was removed, an open border materialised (see Chapter Three). In the space of a few years in the mid-1990s, the border went from being intensely fortified to all but completely open, and EU law was pivotal to this transformation.

For all of the incidental impacts of the Single Market and the welcome provision of EU PEACE and INTERREG funding, the guiding principles of EU law have also been adaptable to the needs of the peace process (Godson, 2005, p 484). Anti-discrimination law is highly developed within the EU legal order; it is of central importance to the functioning of the Single Market that Member States not be able to put rules in place that openly or furtively discriminate against goods, services, capital or individuals from other Member States (McCrudden et al, 2004, p 364). Therefore, when affirmative action rules were put in place to address the historic under-representation

---

[1]   *R (Miller) v Secretary of State for Exiting the European Union* [2017] UKSC 5, [129].

of Catholics in the police force in Northern Ireland under the Patten Reforms,[2] there was a risk that these rules would breach EU law regarding non-discrimination in employment. The EU, however, rapidly provided exemptions to enable police reforms in Northern Ireland to proceed (Council Directive 2000/78/EC, Article 15). The Northern Ireland courts consequently accepted that this provision blocked any legal challenge to these reforms under fair employment legislation (which was based on EU law).[3] In short, the limited mention in the GFA of Ireland's and the UK's shared EU membership underplays its significant role in drawing together both parts of the island of Ireland.

There is, however, a dual risk in Brexit that the EU's commitment is, in some respects, underestimated and, in others, taken for granted by the UK government. Other long-standing principles of EU activity (the "Interlaken Principles") maintain that it will prioritise internal integration and autonomy over deals with non-member states (De Clercq, 1987). The UK government takes little account of this when it insists that the special provisions that the EU has so far been willing to extend for Northern Ireland will be superseded by future negotiations on the post-Brexit UK–EU relationship, which will 'achieve a partnership that is so close as to not require specific measures in relation to Northern Ireland' (Davis, 2018). The special provisions for Northern Ireland that we examine in the chapters ahead represent more than a place-holding deal (a 'backstop', as the UK government likes to call them). They represent a major concession by the EU in light of the rules of EU law, and one that it might be unwilling to rethink when it comes to future negotiations.

---

[2] *Police (Northern Ireland) Act 2000*, section 46(1).

[3] *In re Parsons Application for Judicial Review* [2003] NICA 20, [8] (Lord Carswell).

Re-bordering?

The Brexit campaign

For decades, Northern Ireland's place within the EU has been understood through the lens of Nationalist and Unionist preoccupations with Northern Ireland's constitutional status. However, positions on Europe were, at least up to the Brexit referendum, complex and fluid. Unionism is often portrayed as instinctively Eurosceptic. As a set of political beliefs based on the defence of the UK's sovereignty over Northern Ireland, the pooling of authority together with other member states in EU institutions seemed to carry an existential threat for many Unionists. There have nonetheless been recurrent bouts of engagement with the EU by various Unionist leaders. Nationalism has often been just as divided in its approach to the EU. John Hume was an early adopter, coming to see the EU as attractive for precisely the same reasons that some Unionists were repelled: Europe offered a means to dilute the UK's sovereignty, and meant that the nation state was a concept that was 'dead and gone'. Others were not so sure. As the socialist Republican Bernadette McAliskey famously retorted, she had not yet had her nation state (Meehan, 2000, p 88). This once summed up the position of Sinn Féin, too.

The battles in Northern Ireland during the 2016 Brexit referendum had little to do with David Cameron's renegotiation of the UK's place in the EU. Divisions between the DUP and Sinn Féin over the EU hardened because Northern Ireland's place in the EU became a proxy for something deeper about Northern Ireland's constitutional status. Since the GFA of 1998 (and stretching back to the Anglo-Irish Agreement of 1985), Northern Ireland has been held in a constitutional balance: part of the UK, but connected to the remainder of Ireland. For Brexit's DUP backers, withdrawal from the EU was about tying Northern Ireland more closely into the UK, and much of their campaign focused on the UK as a whole. Only Brexit, Nigel

Dodds (2016) told Westminster, could deliver 'control over our sovereignty, over our borders … [and] over our finances'. Arlene Foster, sometimes said to be less committed to Brexit than her party's Westminster MPs, gave high-profile interviews during the campaign saying that the peace process was not based upon the EU 'in any way' (Foster, 2016). For their part, Sinn Féin's opposition to Brexit during the campaign was less a conversion towards unstinting support for the EU than a direct concern that Brexit 'would harden partition' (*Question Time* – Kearney, 2016).

Ireland and Northern Ireland's place in the Brexit process

The formal process of Brexit got underway on 29 March 2017 with the UK government's initiation of the EU withdrawal procedure (*Treaty on European Union*, Article 50). The UK government insisted at the time that the UK's withdrawal from the EU and future relationship should be negotiated in parallel (Davis, 2017a). By the early summer of 2017, it was clear that this would not be the case; even had the EU Commission (as lead negotiators for the EU) desired such an approach, the remaining EU Member States exerted powerful influence over the EU's priorities (Armstrong, 2017, pp 257–9). The Irish border's prominence in the negotiations that followed should have come as little surprise; the EU's Chief Brexit Negotiator, Michel Barnier, had assured a joint session of the Dáil Éireann and Seanad Éireann in May 2017 that not only would issues of Ireland and Northern Ireland be one of his priorities, but 'in this negotiation Ireland's interest will be the Union's interest' (Barnier, 2017).

These ongoing negotiations are also impacting upon Northern Ireland politics. As an outline deal on Irish issues came into focus in December 2017, it addressed issues such as the 'all-island economy', 'regulatory alignment' and even the possibility of Ireland being reunified within the EU without the need for the EU's 'accession' process by which new members join (*Treaty on*

European Union, Article 49). Without these elements, the EU was clear, there would be no deal (Joint Report, 2017, paras 42–56). However, the DUP became concerned that rather than binding Northern Ireland more closely into the UK, these terms would actually underline its constitutional difference, and perhaps set it on the path towards reunification. In the words of DUP deputy leader Nigel Dodds:

> [I]f as a result of the Brexit negotiations for instance there was to be any suggestion that Northern Ireland would be treated differently, in a way for instance that we were part of a customs union and a single market and the rest of the UK wasn't – if there was anything like the EU's definition of the backstop arrangements that was agreed in December – for us that would be a red line, which we would vote against the Government. (Grimson, 2018)

Given the current balance of power at Westminster, in which Theresa May's minority Conservative administration is reliant on the DUP for support, the terms by which Northern Ireland and the Irish border are covered in the Brexit deal have become central to the shape of Brexit. This situation makes brinkmanship inevitable. Whereas Michel Barnier's EU Task Force presented their draft of how the December 2017 Joint Report could be embodied in a legal text in March 2018 (EU Task Force, 2018a), the UK government has yet to give legal form to its counter-proposals. The UK's position, indeed, changes almost daily. It has to – Brexit can mean anything, and keep as many factions as possible happy, for as long as it does not take specific legal form. As soon as hard choices are made, some of Theresa May's parliamentary support base will be disappointed. However, the clock is ticking towards Brexit in March 2019, and with frantic last-minute negotiations comes the risk of a complete collapse in talks over the issue of Northern Ireland.

Conclusion

Seamus Heaney returned repeatedly to a poem by W.R. Rodgers on Armagh in his thinking about the tangle of identities in the Atlantic Islands, and in Northern Ireland in particular: 'There is a through-otherness about Armagh, Of tower and steeple, Up on the hill are the arguing graves of the kings, And below are the people'. What Heaney took from Rodgers was how untidily Armagh fitted into the conflicting narratives about Ireland as the island's ecclesiastical capital for both Catholics and Protestants. He sought the replication of that sort of shared space elsewhere (Heaney, 2002, p 396). The progressive phases of de-bordering Ireland at the end of the 20th century seemed to give life to this idea, as the GFA, the Common Travel Area and EU membership exerted their cumulative impact. At the dawn of the new millennium, all of Ireland seemed destined to become some grand Armagh or, at least, the other side of the border seemed set to become a less alien and forbidding space (Kearney, 2010, pp 53–4).

When the UK government talks of 'no return to the borders of the past' (HM Treasury, 2017, p 4) it at once conjures up and seeks to dispel memories of watchtowers and militarised patrols. However, writing personally, Theresa May (2018a) also insists that 'any deal with the EU must protect our precious Union'. Brexit places Ireland and the UK on opposite sides of a negotiating table, with Northern Ireland as a key concern. There is a profound risk in such circumstances that Ireland could be presented not as acting as a co-guarantor of the peace process, but as manoeuvring in an international organisation to 'coerce' an end of partition (Barrington, 1957, p 390), stoking age-old Unionist fears and grievances. Only by understanding Brexit's key impacts for Northern Ireland can we confront such imagined demons. That is the task that the rest of this book undertakes.

THREE

Trade

To provide UK business with guarantees of full and equal access to the single market without equal acceptance of EU regulatory structures would require not so much a skilled negotiating team as a fairy godmother specialised in trade law. (Martin Donnelly, Former Permanent Secretary of the Department for International Trade, 2018)

Introduction

Prior to Brexit, shared membership of the European Union (EU) had eliminated most major restrictions upon the trade in goods and services between Northern Ireland and Ireland. A 'frictionless' or 'open' border has existed since the completion of the EU Single Market in the 1990s, without customs checks or the associated infrastructure. Since the Brexit vote, the future of arrangements at this border has been uncertain. This chapter asks what is so 'special' about the EU Customs Union and the Single Market, and considers to what extent the future trade relationship outlined in the Phase 1 Joint Report of December

2017 compensates for being out of the Customs Union and the Single Market. In that report, the UK government pledged a baseline of regulatory alignment with EU law (at least in terms of Northern Ireland) to facilitate cross-border trade in Ireland. This chapter examines the UK government's subsequent proposals and assesses whether they can satisfy both the commitments that the UK has made to the EU and the 'red lines' that it has set for itself: no land border between Ireland and Northern Ireland; trade that is 'as frictionless as possible'; but also no membership of the Single Market and the Customs Union.

The borders of the past

Friction: less trade

One point frequently raised to suggest that keeping the Northern Ireland–Ireland border 'soft' will be achievable is that a border currently exists for what David Davis describes as 'customs and excise purposes' (Sparrow, 2018). However, the shape of that border in 2018 is fundamentally different from what those living in Northern Ireland and Ireland remember as a 'hard border' – a policed partition that existed for a period of almost 70 years.

The establishment of the Irish Free State in 1922, and the Northern Ireland Parliament's decision to not join the Free State, created an international border between what had been counties within a single jurisdiction (see Chapter Two). By 1925, a formal, permanent border between Northern Ireland and Ireland was established via an intergovernmental agreement signed by the Westminster, Stormont and Dublin Parliaments – and that agreement was filed with the League of Nations on 8 February 1926, making it a border not only for intra-UK and Irish purposes, but also under international law (Agreement Between Great Britain and the Irish Free State, amending and supplementing the Treaty of December 6, 1921).

The consequence of the severing of the Free State from the UK was that a single economic area was transformed into two separate trading entities. The primary effect of this was in the area of customs duties: while the UK and the Free State may have initially charged identical tariffs on imports and exports, their trade policy did not stay the same, and any differences in customs tariffs set on products moving between the Free State and the UK resulted in customs declarations being levied. In practice, this led to goods being smuggled across the border to avoid having to pay customs charges, or to benefit from the differences among products made in either jurisdiction (Denton and Fahey, 1993, p 51).

Custom duties/tariffs, or taxes charged on goods that are imported, have historically been very common in international trade, and with the establishment of the Free State in 1923, customs controls – to ensure appropriate duties were paid on those imported goods – were established. The fact that the Free State and Northern Ireland used to be one state was recognised in the legislation governing trade and customs controls between the two parties to some extent; for instance, 'farm produce carried by a farmer' was not subject to tariffs or custom controls when moving across the border, which was a recognition that many farms operated in both jurisdictions and this should continue unhindered insofar as possible (Denton and Fahey, 1993, p 21). We would now call these arrangements – exemption of checks and charges on certain products – an 'Ireland–Northern Ireland Free Trade Agreement'. Until the 1960s, however, such arrangements were less formal, involving 'mirrored' domestic policies rather than international trade treaties.[1]

The agricultural exemption granted in 1923 did not result in a soft border. Even farmers transporting agricultural products had to complete administrative processes to benefit from this exemption, and cross-border tariffs remained applicable to some

---

[1] This pattern of informal and reciprocal arrangements between the UK and Ireland is something of a hallmark of the countries' relationship (see Chapter Two).

agricultural products. 'Ordinary merchandise' was subject to both tariffs and other restrictions, such as import and export by 'approved routes' only (Denton and Fahey, 1993, p 22). Where the differences in tariffs set by the Free State and the UK were significant, the policing of the border also tended to increase as smuggling was made more attractive. Differences in excise (a tax/duty on manufactured goods at their point of production, usually collected at the border) rates similarly inspired smuggling to avoid declarations and payments at the border. A particularly fraught period arrived in the 1930s, when a 'trade war' (known as the Anglo-Irish Tariff Wars) resulted in the requirement for agricultural products to be checked and in a substantial increase in the tariffs charged on steel and coal (Denton and Fahey, 1993, p 37).[2]

Although the 'trade war' eased by 1938, the Second World War once again encouraged cross-border smuggling, not least because economic and social conditions in the Republic, which remained 'neutral' in the war, were significantly better than those in Northern Ireland (Denton and Fahey, 1993, pp 51, 59–60). One further factor was differences in banned products in the respective jurisdictions; for example, Ireland's legislation prohibiting contraceptives resulted in approximately 50 years of smuggling of condoms across the border (Cloatre and Enright, 2017, p 471).

Facilitating trade

The tariff wars slowly faded from the minds of policymakers in the post-war era, and 1965 saw the conclusion of the Anglo-Irish Free Trade Agreement. This committed the Republic of Ireland to progressively reduce its duties against UK products

---

[2] The key piece of UK legislation was the *Irish Free State (Special Duties) Act 1932*, which set duty rates of up to 100% on all Irish Free State goods, including agriculture.

over a period of 10 years and committed the UK to removing all import restrictions on Irish goods by 1966. The agreement resulted in a 'softening' of the border, but it remained very much in existence for economic purposes. The 1960s, of course, also saw the beginnings of the conflict in Northern Ireland, and by the 1970s, the border was marked not only by customs checks, but also by military checkpoints (Smith, 2016).

The next big shift in the degree of smuggling and border policing came when the UK and Ireland both joined the European Economic Community (EEC) in 1973. While EEC membership prevented the introduction of new tariffs between the two countries and therefore reduced the customs-related work taking place at the border, it also introduced the Common Agricultural Policy (CAP) and its farming subsidies in both countries. This led to an entirely new form of 'border fraud', whereby declarations surrounding the quantity, type or weight of agricultural products were falsified to claim fraudulent CAP 'refunds', and so checks on agricultural products were once more increased at the border (Denton and Fahey, 1993, pp 129–30).

However, EEC membership also saw the introduction of measures that resulted in *less* potential for border controls, namely, similar technical standards on products. Technical regulations on products had not historically been the cause of the bulk of delays at the border between Northern Ireland and Ireland, but as the volume of such regulations (for health and safety or environmental purposes) increased in the 1980s, there was potential for a burdensome system of regulatory checks to develop. However, EEC membership meant that products moving between the UK and Ireland did not have to be checked for compliance with EEC regulations (Craig and De Burca, 2015, ch 17).

The 'economic border' between Northern Ireland and Ireland prior to 1993 basically amounted to a hard customs border. The UK and Ireland operated distinct customs and tax regimes, and this required declarations and checks, which were primarily directed at preventing the smuggling of goods. Customs guards have related stories of checking livestock at the border to prevent animal carcasses being used to smuggle alcohol, and checking passenger vehicles for cigarette smuggling (Denton and Fahey, 1993, p 154). Given that the establishment of the Irish Free State coincided with the creation of the Common Travel Area (see Chapter Two), which permitted the free movement of Irish and UK nationals for most everyday purposes, these economic barriers were the most significant obstacles to free flows across the border.

Trade under the European Single Market

Making a single market

The so-called 'completion' of the EU's Single Market project in 1992 had notable consequences for the border between Northern Ireland and Ireland. Explaining why requires discussion of what the EU's Single Market aims to achieve, and to what extent that 'aim' was achieved by the end of 1992. Countries pass through multiple stages when attempting to reduce the number of trade restrictions between them (Belassa, 2013). The first stage in 'integrating' the economies of two countries is concluding a 'simple' free trade agreement (FTA) (simple because of its coverage, not because it will be legible to anyone other than trade lawyers).

An FTA operates where at least two countries abolish custom duties on their 'shared' border. In other words, when a shipment of a product like milk moves from country A to country B, country B does not charge any taxes on the milk being imported, and vice versa.

What if we now introduce Country C, which has sold its milk to country A? Unless it is also part of the FTA, its milk will not move freely between country B and country A; there will be an import charge when it enters country A and another import charge when it moves from country A to country B.

Only goods produced *in* countries A and B consequently benefit from the FTA and its reduced or abolished customs duties. Goods moving within the FTA between country A and country B are subject to 'rules of origin', which define where the good is 'from' – where it was created or significantly modified – and so what customs duties are applicable to it. As discussed, Ireland and the UK operated an 'informal' FTA from 1923, reducing customs duties outside of the context of the 'trade war', and in 1965, they formalised this FTA.

Figure 1: A free trade area

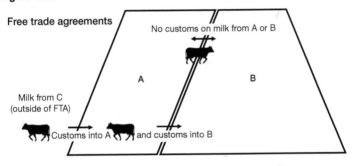

The next stage in economic integration is the creation of a 'customs union'. This is an addition to the FTA. It is formed when countries A and B, already in an FTA with each other, now agree that they would like to apply a single set of rules and tariffs to their *external* borders. In other words, when country C now wishes to sell its milk to either country A or B, those countries will charge the same import taxes on that milk – and once the milk is in either country A or B, it can also freely move to the other country.

We now encounter country D, with no FTA with country A or B, but that wishes to form one with country A because it produces computers that it would like to export to country A at a low tariff. Meanwhile, country A produces bicycles that it would really like to export to country D at a low tariff. It makes sense for countries D and A to conclude an FTA as they clearly have something to offer each other. However, country A can no longer conclude such an FTA on its own because its tariff on country D's computers is determined not only by itself, but also by country B. A customs union must therefore have, as a logical consequence, one external *trade policy*.

Figure 2: A customs union

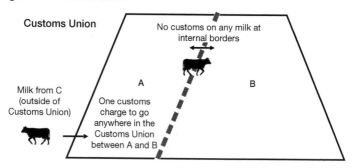

What will the group of countries inside the FTA do whenever an outside country wishes to send products into the trade area? In our example, the external trade policy would cover the negotiation of countries B and A with country D. Country B might have an interest in being able to export bananas at a lower tariff while country A is interested in lowering its bicycle export costs. As countries A and B represent a bigger market than country D, they are likely to be able to exert some pressure on country D in negotiations. This might mean that country D gets less out of the deal for its bicycle, banana and computer industries and consumers, but it still ultimately gets access to country A and B's FTA.

This very simple overview covers the two most common stages of economic integration. While the EU has completed both these stages, it has also gone beyond them (European Commission, 2016). The 1957 Treaty of Rome established Stage

One; since then, the charging of duties on products from the Member States at the EU's internal borders has gradually become prohibited (*Treaty Establishing the European Economic Community*, 1957, Articles 12–15). It also completed Stage Two in 1968, establishing the Customs Union – of which the UK and Ireland have been members since 1973, alongside all other Member States and Monaco. However, the EU's integration project is about much more than simply having no border tariffs and shared trade rules; it provides the institutional architecture that enforces and supervises such rules that differentiates a 'common market' (or Stage Three of integration) from a simpler FTA or customs union.

The EU's common market project

Since the 1957 Treaty of Rome, the EU has had a goal to create a 'common market'. However, the simple negative provisions in the Treaty of Rome – declaring that Member States will not impose restrictions on the movement of goods, services, capital or people – did very little to actually encourage the development of a functional internal market. We leave the discussion of people (see Chapter Four) as our primary interest here is trade between Northern Ireland and Ireland in the context of the EU's efforts to ensure genuine free movement in goods.

Prior to the 1980s, there was very little EEC law governing internal *regulations* on goods, services and capital. A product, in other words, could probably cross a border without incurring a fee, but it might incur a sales tax or, indeed, a restriction on sale based on health and safety, cultural differences such as the legal age to drink, or other grounds. These problems, rooted in the combined facts that the Member States did not have to accept products with different standards from other Member States and the lack of general rules setting identical standards, were extremely difficult to change. The EU's decision-making structures were heavily biased towards the interests of individual

Member States, who could – and did – block proposals to establish common standards and regulations if their national interest was at issue. Domestic lobbying on matters of trade significantly limited the extent to which the EEC could achieve a genuine EEC-wide market in which all products were in direct competition with each other, regardless of origin.

It took an economic downturn for attitudes to change, largely at the behest of the UK and Prime Minister Margaret Thatcher. She sent an envoy, Baron Cockfield, to the EU Commission in an attempt to revive the common market project. Commissioner Cockfield's White Paper proposed an extensive number of *positive* laws that the EU would need to adopt to actually create (or 'complete') what he called the 'single market'. This led to the EEC adopting its first new treaty in over 30 years – the Single European Act of 1986 – which promised the completion of the Single Market by the end of 1992.

The Single European Act introduced both 'negative' and 'positive' rules, as well as an overarching power for the EU to create new legislation where this was necessary for the 'establishment and functioning of the internal market', which enabled integration to move faster. This new power, found in Article 100a of the EC Treaty, stopped Member State vetoes on any and all matters that they proclaimed to be of 'national interest'. Instead, the system functioned under 'qualified majority voting', meaning that a single Member State opposing a legislative measure was no longer enough to stop it from taking effect. In other words, the relaxation of the Member States' veto 'grip' meant that common standards and regulations that assist the creation of the 'single' or 'internal' market are adopted with significantly greater speed and ease.

The EU's Single Market in 1992

The EU itself estimates that by the end of 1992, 90% of the pre-existing issues plaguing the 'internal market', as identified in

Baron Cockfield's White Paper, were resolved (Maciejewski and Dancourt, 2017). For instance, EEC regulations harmonising customs declaration paperwork in 1987 (EEC Commission Regulation No 1062/87) meant that goods started moving across EU internal borders – including the Ireland–Northern Ireland border – with significantly greater ease and at a reduced cost (Hayward, 2017). The free movement of services remains the most incomplete aspect of the Single Market, but it is less significant to the Ireland–Northern Ireland border because of the Common Travel Area's operation. With the Single Market in *goods* finally completed in 1993, customs posts on the Irish border became redundant and could be removed.

What, then, defines the 'Single Market in goods', and why did this development remove the need for border checks when being in the EEC as an FTA and a customs union, between 1973 and 1992, did not? The decisive factor is the extent to which technical regulations on trade have multiplied since the 1990s – and what this will mean for trade post-Brexit. Returning to the border of 1973 or 1992 is not an option post-Brexit. The EU's external borders now police a multitude of technical regulations that have evolved with the 'internal market' since 1992. As we have seen, the primary 'checks' taking place at Ireland's land border up until 1992 were for customs charges, for excise payments and to prevent smuggling due to product restrictions. Following Brexit, however, the UK and the EU will be able to operate different customs and tax policies, but also different regulatory policies. If this happens, a 'hard' border will be needed to process customs and tax declarations, and also to check products crossing the border for their compliance with their destination's product regulations.

It is the latter process that would cause the most substantial border delays; customs and tax obligations can be largely electronically discharged, but product regulations will often require actual checks to take place (with all of the associated physical infrastructure). This is particularly the case with agricultural products; the so-called sanitary and phytosanitary (SPS) measures that the EU applies in principle require all goods from *outside* of the EU to be subjected to extensive checks as soon as they arrive at an EU border to ensure that they meet EU health and safety standards (European Commission, no date[a]). Under World Trade Organization (WTO) law, if the EU relaxes those standards to facilitate trade across the Northern Ireland border, it would have to relax those standards for *all* its trading partners – and consequently amend its own founding treaties as most of the commitments regarding the Single Market would no longer be achievable. Unsurprisingly, there is no chance of it doing so.

The fact that products (agricultural and otherwise) may need to be inspected before crossing the border between Northern Ireland and Ireland post-Brexit is therefore a consequence of the development that the EU has undergone since 1973. A mutual 'understanding' rooted in aligned domestic laws, which the UK and Ireland maintained before 1965, will no longer cut it.

Brexit: what will change?

Red lines

Key to determining how the situation at the Northern Ireland border will change post-Brexit is the UK government's negotiation 'red lines'. Theresa May insists that exiting the EU *will* mean leaving both the EU Customs Union and the Single Market. This means leaving behind the 'architecture' that builds mutual trust in the EU's rules and standards enabling goods to move freely between countries. If these 'red lines' are maintained, the European Commission will have no jurisdiction to investigate the UK's compliance with EU law, and there will be no more enforcement of EU law in the UK by the European Commission or the Court of Justice of the EU (CJEU). Whatever makes up the UK's trade policy, these will be domestic concepts rather than EU ones, and will not be subject to the CJEU's interpretations.

We will now explore the consequences of the UK's 'red lines' for the border in Northern Ireland: first, considering what changes if the UK and the EU are no longer in a customs union together; and, second, considering what changes if the UK leaves the Single Market.

Leaving the Customs Union

So far, the consequences of leaving the EU Customs Union have not been highlighted by the discussions of the pre-1993 and post-1993 border, for the very simple reason that that border has never before been an external border of the *EU*. As the UK and Ireland joined the EEC at the same time, the border between them has always been an 'internal' EU border rather than an 'external' border.

Brexit changes this. Ireland will become an entry point to the EU for goods travelling from Northern Ireland, and that means that goods leaving Northern Ireland and crossing into Ireland will be entering the EU Customs Union for the first time. What this means varies to a significant extent depending on what kind of relationship the UK and the EU (as a whole) will have following Brexit; however, given the Prime Minister's insistence that the UK will leave 'the Customs Union', it is possible to make several notes on the customs checks that will be needed in future.

The customs duties set by the UK and the EU vis-a-vis each other will be regulated through an FTA. The current state of negotiations suggests that the EU and UK will agree, if nothing else, on concluding an FTA that eliminates all tariff barriers. As such, it does not look likely that there will be a return to the pre-1973 border in Northern Ireland: customs duties are not likely to need collecting for products that move from the UK into Ireland or from Ireland into Northern Ireland. What is key, however, is that it applies to goods *originating* in the UK and in the EU. Once the Ireland–Northern Ireland border becomes an external EU border, it is also where products from third countries may potentially enter the EU – and those may have duties to be collected. Duties on goods imported from non-EU countries are currently collected when goods first enter the UK or Ireland, and they will ordinarily do so at (air)ports, thus leaving the Northern Ireland border unaffected; however, that stops being an option when the UK itself is no longer in the EU and the Northern Ireland border becomes a point of 'EU entry' for all goods that arrive in the UK from elsewhere.

At present, an LCD TV being imported from India to either a port in Ireland or Northern Ireland will be charged a 14% duty there, and then can go anywhere in the EU without attracting a further charge, including across the land border. Following Brexit, however, let us say that the UK operates a tariff of only 5% and the EU maintains its 14% tariff. An LCD TV from India arriving in Belfast will thus attract a 5% duty – and can then be driven across the land border for use or sale in Ireland. Without customs posts at the land border, the EU's duty on that Indian TV will simply not be collected, which would undoubtedly attract complaints from those traders who *are* faced with the EU external tariff when sending a TV directly to Amsterdam, for instance.

As discussed earlier, EU Member States have a common external trade policy. Third countries, like China, which sign trade agreements do so with the EU, and the same 'tariff reductions' apply in all Member States. Brexit, however, carves the UK out of that system; therefore, we may arrive in a situation where the UK and the EU both have trade agreements with the same third country but the tariffs negotiated on products from that third country are *not* the same for the UK and the EU.

In a scenario where neither the UK nor the EU have a trade agreement with a third country, there are still potential problems. Where there are no trade agreements between states or customs unions, tariffs are based on the WTO's so-called tariff 'schedules' (basically, lists of charges on different goods). Each state as well as the EU maintains such a list with the WTO. Currently, the UK does not have a separate list of its own as it is part of the EU's Single Market. Post-Brexit, the UK's schedules may need to be reconsidered. Duplicating the EU's terms for the UK may be unattractive to many WTO members, who may wish to give the UK a significantly different membership deal than they did the 500-million-consumer EU Single Market. Even if the schedule is duplicated for the UK, it is likely to change over time, which means that third-country goods are likely to experience different tariffs upon moving from the UK into the EU, and vice versa. This will require paperwork and checks at the external EU–UK borders, which will include the Northern Ireland border.

Unfortunately, this is only the beginning of the potential reasons for delays at the border; the real complications arise in relation to complex manufactured goods and an area of trade law that only specialists consider but that has suddenly become a significant buzzword in political circles: rules of origin.

Due to how global supply chains operate, a product that 'arrives' in the EU from the UK might, in reality, have been sourced from a variety of worldwide locations, only being 'completed' in the UK before moving into the EU. Where is such a product from? This might sound like a silly question, but it is a crucial one for determining what tariffs need to be charged on that product at the border. FTAs all have their own formulae for calculating so-called 'rules of origin', determining where a product has undergone its 'last substantial transformation' for the purposes of applying a customs duty to it.

An example provided to the Business, Energy and Industrial Strategy Select Committee by Mike Hawes, Chief Executive of the Society of Motor Manufacturers and Traders, will make this clearer:

The average car made in the UK purchases 44% of its components from UK suppliers, in other words 56% from abroad. For the purposes of free trade agreements, we look at something called originating content. That means, of that 44% that you are buying from your UK suppliers, how much actually comes from the UK, bearing in mind the supply chain, tier two, will still be buying from Europe, Asia and elsewhere. We are doing some work on that figure at the moment, and it is somewhere between 20% and 25%, which is a long way from the 55% to 60% threshold you would need to qualify for any free trade agreement…. to move from where we currently are – let us say 20% to 25% originating content – to 60% will take many years. There is not necessarily the capability here in the UK. (House of Commons Business, Energy and Industrial Strategy Committee, 2017)

The way around this is 'cumulation', whereby countries agree to allow components originating from each other's jurisdictions to count towards the 'transformation' threshold. If applicable to any future UK–EU trade deal, parts of a car produced in the EU would count towards a car being 'made' in the UK. However, cumulation becomes more complex in truly global supply chains, where rules on cumulation would need to be agreed with a wide variety of third-country trading partners by both the UK and the EU. Such 'diagonal cumulation', between a variety of trading partners, will require a lot of trade agreement coordination between the UK and the EU in the absence of EU Customs Union membership (Imana, 2009; World Customs Organisation 2012; Lowe, 2016).

It should be stressed that even if the respective rules are, in practice, *not different*, unless there is a mutual, legally binding commitment to operate identical rules, it is likely that controls will be reinstated again at Ireland's land border simply to *verify* that identical rules are being applied – or to be able to act quickly *if* the UK diverges from EU rules. This is the difference between being in *a* customs union with the EU, and thus committing to operating identical rules and having an enforcement and oversight mechanism to enforce that commitment, and operating a separate customs policy that happens to overlap with the EU's rules.

Leaving the Single Market

The Single Market is the most advanced example of economic integration between countries in the world. There is extensive harmonisation of standards in EU law, but, importantly, even when there is *no* harmonisation, the EU operates on principles of 'mutual recognition', with only limited exceptions. As a consequence, once a product is legally sold in one Member State, it should be sellable in all other Member States, unless there are overriding specific reasons that permit a particular Member State to block its sale.[3] This combination of harmonised EU rules and Member States' mutual recognition of each other's rules means that products simply do not have to be checked at the border.

In the rare situation where a product produced in Member State A can, for legitimate overriding reasons, not be sold in Member State B, this can be controlled *within* the Member States, rather than at the border – or at the point of sale, rather than at the point of import. Borders, consequently, might be there as geographical landmarks within the EU, but they no longer serve a trade purpose. The fact that all Member States continue to operate restrictions on the importation of alcohol and cigarettes above a set volume is not a matter that is policed at any of the land borders. Where there are suspicions of smuggling of products like alcohol and cigarettes, or of the movement of otherwise *illegal* goods (such as cocaine), this has, post-1993,

---

[3] C-120/78 *Rewe-Zentral AG v Bundesmonopolverwaltung für Branntwein* EU:C:1979:42.

become a matter for regular police investigation. Where border agents continue to operate, it is at the EU's external land borders and (air)ports, where goods arriving from *outside* of the EU still require extensive verification before being allowed into the Single Market.

That said, there is more to the 'Single Market' than the rules that make up EU law. Rules only become meaningful in complex trade relations when there is significant mutual trust that they will be abided by. If country A promises that it definitely produces milk in the same way that country B does, that only becomes a meaningful commitment if country B can somehow 'trust' that country A is doing that – and in international trade, trust is heavily contingent on the ability to *check* and *ensure* that the rules are applied. We can see this clearly in the EU's proposals for the Ireland Protocol in the Withdrawal Agreement: the rules are the starting point, but the enforcement of those rules is equally important.

Within the EU, there is an extensive architecture which ensures that EU law is interpreted and enforced in the same way, that there is appropriate supervision of commitments made by EU Member States, and that all the Member States 'sincerely cooperate' to ensure that EU laws function (*Treaty on European Union*, Article 4(3)).[4] The EU institutions, and their ability to hold each other and the Member States to account if they do not comply, are what build the trust necessary to abandon border controls. Compatible and mutually recognised rules, in other words, are the beginning of *not needing border checks* at EU internal borders; the full extent of institutional and administrative cooperation and integration that make up the EU Single Market are an equally essential part of it (European Commission, 2018a).

Post-Brexit, the UK will move into a separate regulatory regime for all products, agricultural or otherwise. What this will mean in practice depends on what kind of 'new' FTA the

---

[4]   C-397-403/01 *Pfeiffer v Deutsches Rotes Kreuz* EU:C:2004:584.

UK and the EU conclude. However, both the EU and the UK concede that even the very 'best', most expansive FTA will not be as all-encompassing as the EU Single Market (European Council, 2018; May, 2018b). There will be a 'hit' in terms of coverage – trade in services will likely become subject to many more restrictions than currently under EU rules – but there will also be a hit in terms of 'trading freedom' even for areas included in a future FTA. Without CJEU and European Commission oversight of whatever product rules the UK operates, the EU cannot simply accept them into its territory: it will need checks to ensure that they meet the EU's standards. Unless the UK and the EU either shift their negotiating positions or come up with some radical new solutions for complying with their global trade obligations, regulatory checks at Northern Ireland's land border will resurface post-Brexit.

UK proposals for 'solving' the Northern Ireland border

Starting points for negotiations

The EU's consistent negotiating position has been that leaving the Single Market and the EU Customs Union are UK 'red lines', not EU red lines, and the EU is very much open to the UK pursuing European Economic Area (EEA) membership and *a* customs union that will function largely in the same way as the EU Customs Union does for Member States. The UK has, however, rejected both of those solutions and the EU, after significant lobbying from Ireland, has therefore batted the ball back into the UK's court and asked it to propose solutions for Northern Ireland given that the EU's 'solutions' have been deemed unacceptable (Connelly, 2018a, pp 180–8).

The UK has obliged in the form of a set of 'Future Partnership' papers on trade and customs, wherein it sets out its vision for both the future EU–UK FTA generally, and what steps will be taken to mitigate the effect of Brexit on the Northern Ireland border specifically (HM Treasury et al, 2017). Here, too, the

UK has developed a set of red lines, which are essential to understanding the solutions that it has proposed:

- There will be *no physical infrastructure* at the Northern Ireland border as this would be politically, socially and culturally unacceptable for those living in either Ireland or Northern Ireland, and may bring with it security concerns.
- There will be *no hard border* between Ireland and Northern Ireland.
- There will be *no hard border* between Northern Ireland and Great Britain.

In other words, the UK simultaneously acknowledges that a hard border at the EU's new external front is completely undesirable and commits to avoiding it but also commits to not establishing what might be the obvious *alternative* location for a de facto EU external border: the Irish Sea. As explained earlier, those positions set a seemingly impossible task for the EU: where does it apply its controls on goods coming in from the UK (a third country) to Ireland?

To answer that question, the UK proposes three equally controversial but very different solutions. On the customs front, it offers two alternatives: a 'Maximum Facilitation' ('Max Fac') customs arrangement between the UK and the EU (Option 1); or a so-called 'Customs Partnership' (Option 2). On the 'regulatory standards' front, its position is more abstract but can broadly be described as being focused on 'outcome alignment' in regulation, resulting in mutual recognition of standards (Option 3). We will explore each of these proposals in turn.

Option 1: 'Max Fac'

The UK government has made a concerted pitch for what has become known as the 'Max Fac' arrangement:

A highly streamlined customs arrangement between the UK and the EU, streamlining and simplifying requirements, leaving as few additional requirements on UK–EU trade as possible. This would aim to: continue some of the existing agreements between the UK and the EU; put in place new negotiated and unilateral facilitations to reduce and remove barriers to trade; and implement technology-based solutions to make it easier to comply with customs procedures. (HM Treasury et al, 2017, para 27)

The customs 'Future Partnership' paper establishes in more detail what kinds of solutions, ranging from technological to cooperation agreements, could result in trade *facilitation*. We do not need to consider it in more detail than that, however, because the promises made by both the UK and the EU with regards to the Northern Ireland border are not about *minimising* the level of border checks done; they simply preclude border checks altogether. Max Fac will consequently result in something that has been described in terms of 'as frictionless as possible' a border, but this is not the same thing as 'no physical infrastructure' and 'no hard border'. As the House of Commons Northern Ireland Affairs Committee (NIAC) concluded:

The Committee has heard numerous proposals for how the UK and the EU could ensure customs compliance without physical infrastructure at the border. This is currently the case for enforcement in relation to fuel, alcohol and tobacco. These proposals address the question of compliance through mobile patrols, risk analysis, data-sharing and enforcement measures away from the border. However, we have had no visibility of any technical solutions, anywhere in the world, beyond the aspirational, that would remove the need for physical infrastructure at the border. (NIAC, 2018a, para 82)

Theresa May appears to have conceded as much in her Mansion House speech: 'Option two would be a highly streamlined customs arrangement, where we would jointly agree to implement a range of measures to minimise frictions to trade, together with specific provisions for Northern Ireland' (May, 2018b). However, to date, what those specific provisions for Northern Ireland would be, and how they fulfil all three of the commitments made with regards to borders in Northern Ireland, has not been specified further, beyond maintaining the current policy of treating the island of Ireland as a single agricultural entity and pursuing an exemption for 'small traders'. The latter, of course, will not avoid a border because if there is an exemption, there will also be a rule to be applied, and that rule will require verification to ensure that everyone claiming to be a 'small trader' is actually a 'small trader' (NIAC, 2018a, para 71).

Option 2: the Customs Partnership

Option 2, known as the 'Customs Partnership', has become the foremost option being pursued by UK ministers who are not ardent Brexiteers – perhaps unsurprisingly given the limitations of Max Fac. However, the Customs Partnership is no less ambitious than using technology to try to 'avoid' or 'minimise' a border. The UK has been sparing on the details of what it imagines a Customs Partnership to look like, but the Mansion House speech suggests the following:

> At the border, the UK would mirror the EU's requirements for imports from the rest of the world, applying the same tariffs and the same rules of origin as the EU for those goods arriving in the UK and intended for the EU. By following this approach, we would know that all goods entering the EU via the UK pay the right EU duties, removing the need for customs processes at the UK–EU border.

But, importantly, we would put in place a mechanism so that the UK would also be able to apply its own tariffs and trade policy for goods intended for the UK market. As we have set out previously, this would require the means to ensure that both sides can trust the system and a robust enforcement mechanism. (May, 2018b)

In theory, this appears to satisfy all the UK red lines and the EU–UK mutual 'Northern Ireland' red lines. The problem lies in practice, however, which is that having one country collect duties using another country's tariffs and then refunding traders according to where the goods actually end up as a final destination is not done anywhere in the world. It will require extensive tracking of goods *into* the Single Market, and therefore a lot of EU cooperation to set up a system that is significantly more awkward than the Single Market.

The EU has dismissed the Customs Partnership proposal as it currently stands as being unrealistic, not least of all because of the short timescale in which it would have to be up and running and its overly costly and burdensome operation for both traders and Member States because of the endless 'refund' claims and transport monitoring that it would involve (Parker, 2018).

The Customs Partnership is also the 'customs' option that has attracted severe criticism from within the Conservative Party. A crunch cabinet meeting in May 2018 was intended to result in the 'adoption' of the Customs Partnership as the option to be pursued, but it actually resulted in the cabinet agreeing only that, as currently proposed, the model is unworkable. Minister Greg Clark conceded that getting both the UK and the EU ready to operate the Customs Partnership will take, at the very least, five years beyond the 'exit' day transition period (BBC, 2018a). However, given that (as NIAC strongly suggests) a 'Max Fac' solution also is unlikely to be ready for deployment by the end of the transition period, this is likely to be a lesser factor in opposition to the Customs Partnership. Instead, Boris Johnson made clear that it is the long-term consequences of being in the Customs Partnership itself that are causing the opposition:

It's totally untried and would make it very, very difficult to do free trade deals. If you have the new customs partnership, you have a crazy system whereby you end up collecting the tariffs on behalf of the EU at the UK frontier. If the EU decides to impose punitive tariffs on something the UK wants to bring in cheaply there's nothing you can do.

That's not taking back control of your trade policy, it's not taking back control of your laws, it's not taking back control of your borders and it's actually not taking back control of your money either, because tariffs would get paid centrally back to Brussels. (Doyle, 2018)

Given both of these internal and external restrictions, it seems that the Customs Partnership in its current form is also not the proposal that will find its way into the Withdrawal Agreement and the partnership agreement to prevent a hard border in Northern Ireland. However, on 8 May 2018, the Irish Taoiseach, Leo Varadkar, told the Dáil that EU opposition is primarily to the Customs Partnership proposal in its current form, 'but it is something that perhaps we could make workable' (Houses of the Oireachtas, 2018). In light of the intra-cabinet disagreement on which route to pursue, as well as the EU rejection of both models as currently developed, both 'Max Fac' and the 'Customs Partnership' are being redeveloped by the UK at the time of writing.

Option 3: mutual recognition and/or outcome alignment

Customs duties, however, are only one part of what causes border checks; the remainder, as explained earlier, is made up of product checks that have to do with technical regulations. It might seem as though the problems posed by the UK leaving the EU can be rather more easily resolved here: goods crossing the border will become problematic only if the UK operates *different* technical regulations than the EU. Indeed, the UK government's primary argument in the negotiations on Brexit to date has been that as long as the rules remain identical, or the EU and the UK recognise each other's rules as 'good enough', trade should be able to continue without border checks between the UK and the EU:

> The UK will need to make a strong commitment that its regulatory standards will remain as high as the EU's. That commitment, in practice, will mean that UK and EU regulatory standards will remain substantially similar in the future.
>
> Our default is that UK law may not necessarily be identical to EU law, but it should achieve the same outcomes. In some cases Parliament might choose to pass an identical law – businesses who export to the EU tell us that it is strongly in their interest to have a single set of regulatory standards that mean they can sell into the UK and EU markets.
>
> If the Parliament of the day decided not to achieve the same outcomes as EU law, it would be in the knowledge that there may be consequences for our market access.
>
> And there will need to be an independent mechanism to oversee these arrangements. (May, 2018b)

However, this pitch for 'simple mutual recognition' between the EU and a non-Member State UK significantly underplays the unprecedented achievement that is the Single Market. The type of 'mutual recognition' being asked for by the UK does not even exist between the Member States, where – as Stephen Weatherill (2014) argues persuasively – *exceptions* to mutual recognition still operate under the CJEU's oversight.

Mutual recognition is far from present between the EU and other third countries, not only because third countries operate significantly different rules from the EU, but also because there are limits to the level of 'mutual recognition' that the EU is willing to pursue internationally, where it has less control over how regulatory standards are adopted and enforced than it does within the Single Market (NIAC, 2018a , para 43). Post-Brexit, while the UK might start out with identical rules, it will not start out with identical trust as the Member States do.

Existing examples of 'mutual recognition' that the EU has accepted in international trade agreements are rare. For one thing, in the EU's FTAs, what is normally called 'mutual recognition' refers only to so-called conformity assessment exercises, whereby the EU recognises assessments from approved authorities in that third country proclaiming that the products being exported to the EU meet the EU's regulatory standards (Institute for Government, 2017). This is a world removed from what the UK Prime Minister asks for in her Mansion House speech, which is effectively the EU recognising that *whatever* the UK adopts as regulatory standards, this will be 'equal' to EU standards.

There are some policy areas in which the EU operates a form of 'recognition' of foreign regulation; however, this comes with significant caveats. These kinds of 'equivalence' decisions, where the EU determines that foreign rules are 'equal' to EU rules, are unilaterally extended by the EU and revocable without any particular appeal rights, as they are in the area of financial services (European Commission, no date[b]). It is difficult to imagine that this type of unilateral one-way recognition of UK standards would be seen as stable enough to avoid having any infrastructure at the Northern Ireland border; after all, the UK's regulations *may* currently guarantee compliance with EU rules but they could stop doing so at any point in time, if 'the Parliament of the day' decided as much. It would be impossible not to reintroduce border controls in those circumstances.

There are specific problems in requesting 'mutual recognition' of agri-food standards in particular. Switzerland was not exempt from EU border controls until, in 2009, it signed the so-called Veterinary Agreement, which commits it to effectively adopting the entire EU acquis on agricultural health and safety, as well as indefinitely updating it (FSVO, 2017). This arrangement permits agriculture to move between Switzerland and the EU but can hardly be described as 'mutual recognition'.

The UK government appears attuned to the importance of the free movement of agri-food on the island of Ireland as it specifically highlights SPS measures as needing resolution to prevent a hard border in Northern Ireland. However, it uses Switzerland as an example of the EU reaching 'deep agreement with near neighbours', only to then ask for something quite different than what Switzerland has: recognition of 'regulatory equivalence' (UK Government, 2017a, paras 55–7). Switzerland, in other words, sets a precedent for something that the UK is not actually willing to agree to and the EU is not offering on 'Swiss' terms.

'Mutual recognition' of equivalent outcomes pursued in the UK, in short, is asking the EU to operate on a level of trust that only exists within the Single Market. Given its insistence that there be no 'cherry-picking' of elements of Single Market membership, it is unsurprising that noises coming from the EU on this proposal of 'outcome alignment' have been sceptical (EU Task Force, 2018b, p 15).

The Phase 1 Joint Report

The art of the deal?

The Phase 1 negotiations centred on three UK proposals, all flawed or at the very least underdeveloped, to avoid a border in Northern Ireland. The EU's response was to set out a clear challenge: either the UK finds ways to make these solutions actually workable, *or* Northern Ireland will have to, in effect, stay in the Customs Union and the Single Market for goods.

In the Joint Report agreed by the negotiators in December 2017, this took the shape of three alternatives to resolving the Northern Ireland border for trade purposes (Joint Report, 2017, para 49). First, ideally, the UK and the EU would like to conclude a future trade arrangement which would mean that there will be no hard border (Option A). If this cannot be achieved, and as we noted earlier, the current 'trade arrangement' proposals do not seem to, then the UK will propose 'island of Ireland' solutions (Option B). It is very difficult to see what these would look like if not 'special status' for Northern Ireland. Northern Ireland could be declared an autonomous customs territory able to strike a trade deal with the EU that prevents a hard border without the participation of the rest of the UK. This is workable – and there are World Trade Organization precedents, such as Macau – but politically unacceptable to the Democratic Unionist Party (DUP) as it would violate the UK's third promise with regards to Northern Ireland borders by establishing one between Northern Ireland and Great Britain.

That brings us to Option C: if all else fails, in paragraph 49, the UK government agreed that the UK will maintain 'full alignment with those rules of the Internal Market and the Customs Union which, now or in the future, support North–South cooperation, the all-island economy and the protection of the 1998 agreement'. This seems to suggest that the UK is promising to effectively adopt EU legislation in all those areas of law that have an impact on *both the all-island economy* and the *Good Friday Agreement's* (GFA's) core content. This explicitly goes *beyond* the GFA as it specifically enumerates three bases for full alignment, namely: (1) North–South cooperation; (2) the all-island economy; and (3) the 1998 agreement. The Joint Report thus seems to require full regulatory alignment with Single Market rules on free movement of both industrial goods and agricultural goods, and a customs union between the UK and the EU that obviates the need for border controls.

Constructive ambiguity

Since December, disputes have broken out between the UK and the EU on what exactly 'full alignment' means and what parts of the UK it applies to; the UK has argued that it means 'outcome alignment', whereas the EU believes that it means adopting the relevant EU acquis (Campbell, J. 2017; Barnier, 2018; House of Commons Exiting the European Union Committee, 2018a, paras 42–50). Furthermore, when the EU's Brexit Task Force drafted its proposals for the Withdrawal Agreement, it set out Option C as applying specifically to Northern Ireland (EU Task Force, 2018a, Protocol on Ireland/Northern Ireland, Article 3). This seems to ignore the terms of paragraph 50, and so does not take account of the UK government's unilateral guarantees to the DUP that no new borders arise between Northern Ireland and Great Britain. The UK government has since maintained, as its DUP backers at Westminster demand, that paragraph 49 of the Joint Report sets out an 'all-UK' solution – meaning that whatever trade arrangement is available to Northern Ireland should be available to the remainder of the UK as well.

In the context of Option C, the EU regards any special solutions for Northern Ireland as exclusive to Northern Ireland, meaning they cannot set a precedent for the remaining 'future partnership' negotiations (eg Joint Report, 2017, para 46). How the UK avoids a border between Great Britain and Northern Ireland has consistently been treated as an 'internal matter' by the EU. It is in that sense perhaps obvious that its proposed Withdrawal Agreement text applies to Northern Ireland (as part of the island of Ireland) alone. This suggestion moved the UK government to a level of outrage proportionate to its current reliance upon the DUP at Westminster. Theresa May declared that no UK prime minister could accept what the EU had put into text – suggesting that Option C will only be acceptable if it applies to the whole of the UK (House of Commons Exiting the European Union Committee, 2018a , para 43). The UK government has since reaffirmed its commitment to the Joint Report, including the backstop solution, but has yet to produce a detailed, alternative version of Option A, B or C that satisfies both its own red lines and those of the EU.

Conclusion

The UK's negotiation positions to date remain mutually exclusive; it is not possible to simultaneously exit both the EU Customs Union and the Single Market and fully avoid a physical border. The desire for no special treatment for Northern Ireland in terms of the EU Customs Union makes this more complicated – the Northern Ireland land border is clearly a distinct issue in the negotiations. To ensure no special treatment for Northern Ireland, the UK as a whole will have to set up highly EU-compliant customs arrangements – not merely a customs agreement, but one that obviates the need for any border controls. The EU does not have such an arrangement with any third country, and were it to establish one with the UK, it would probably require the UK to sign up to the EU regulatory regime but without any particular input into that regulatory regime. This is not just a customs regulatory issue; other questions such as data protection to ensure access to data sharing/information exchange and e-customs systems will also come into play.

Regulatory differences create borders. Differences in agricultural or environmental standards will have a significant impact on import/export ability – not only in the sense of it becoming more expensive, but genuinely in the sense of 'Is it still going to be possible?', as the many mentions of 'chlorine chicken' before select committees made clear over the course of 2016 and 2017 (NIAC, 2018a, para 43).

At present, the UK government promises to put in place appropriate regulations but this is not the same as being legally bound to have those regulations. The EU treaties mandate that those regulations apply within member states. However, given that the UK is aiming to have regulatory independence, another source of law will need to replace the EU treaties but be of an equally binding nature in order to guarantee to the EU that UK products meet the agreed-upon requirements. The future UK–EU trade agreement will consequently require a supervisory authority of some kind, as well as a dispute resolution mechanism – and the more 'open' the borders between the UK and the EU are to be in practice, the more active and expansive those supervisory and dispute resolution mechanisms will need to be to satisfy the EU.

The UK remaining within the EU Single Market and a customs union equivalent to the EU Customs Union after Brexit would therefore be the best outcome in terms of minimising friction at the EU's new external border with Northern Ireland. The UK government currently rejects this option but its proposed solutions do not take account of the EU's need to protect its international obligations with regard to its trading borders, as well as what is technically and practically feasible in the short period before a post-Brexit border regime has to be set up in both the UK and the EU.

In the alternative, a special status for Northern Ireland whereby it – separately from Britain – remains within the EU Single Market and the EU Customs Union would resolve the problems that may arise at the Northern Ireland land border observed earlier. This, of course, would result in a 'border' existing in the Irish Sea, which would then be the point at which the EU's regulatory regime would be applied. Again, the UK government currently rejects this option but has not offered an alternative that can fully avoid physical infrastructure at the Northern Ireland land border (whether at the border or near the border).

In late May, it was reported that David Davis was due to pitch a 'third' model: staying in what *The Times* hilariously reported to be a 'Customs and Regulatory Alignment Period' ('CRAP') until 2023, when Max Fac or a Customs Partnership will be ready (according to Her Majesty's Revenue and Customs [HMRC]) (Wright et al, 2018). *The Times* has since added an 'Implementation' to the title of the pitch – but that does not change the extent to which the original title likely captured how such a proposal is liable to be received by both sceptics at home and in the EU. Under CRA(I)P, the UK would, in effect, be asking for a second transition period between 2020 and 2023 – but only for rules affecting customs and trade.

Instead of full CRA(I)P, on 7 June 2018, the UK ended up pitching what was only a Customs Alignment Period to the EU as a partial 'backstop' solution for Northern Ireland: until alternative arrangements could be made (by the end of 2021 the government suggested), the UK would stay aligned with the EU Custom Union's rules as necessary (Cabinet Office, 2018). The Technical Note setting out this customs 'backstop' proposal suggests that a separate proposal on 'regulatory standards' – and how those will be managed so as to avoid a border – will follow.

Though only a partial solution, does this Customs Alignment Period at least resolve the customs element of the Northern Ireland border problem? Well, yes and no. EU responses to the proposal make clear that in its view, the paragraph 49 'full alignment' setup was never intended to cover the entirety of the UK as this would enable 'cherry-picking' of bits of EU membership and set a precedent that the EU does not want (Connelly, 2018b; EU Task Force, 2018c). However, this is not the only problem that a 'customs and regulatory alignment implementation period' faces as a proposal: it will be staunchly opposed in Westminster by those wishing to make a clean break from the EU as soon as possible. Furthermore, to make matters worse, even if they are assuaged by the fact that this is only a temporary situation, the EU certainly will not be: the conditions in the Joint Report demand a Northern Ireland solution to be there come what may, *not come 2021* (EU Task Force, 2018c).

Something will have to give either on the UK side or the EU side to keep the Northern Ireland land border as it is. To summarise the situation at the end of June 2018, either the UK needs to come up with a workable 'solution' to the border situation or the EU has to accept the UK as a whole staying in the Single Market for goods and the EU Customs Union (though only temporarily, until a workable 'solution' can be found). Who is most likely to budge? Some are hopeful that it will be the EU: a complete version of CRA(I)P, even if ultimately destined to be replaced, may sound like permitting the kind of cherry-picking of the Single Market that the EU has categorically ruled out, but it does not amount to the UK getting to have its cake and eat it. The Protocol proposals do not cover trade in services, which make up the vast majority of the UK's exports to the EU and economy as a whole. A temporary 'UK as a whole stays in', as such, comes with a UK price to pay, is unlikely to be attractive to other EU Member States and pushes the 'real' negotiations on movement of people (which the UK is opposed to) and movement of services (which the EU is opposed to) into the future talks (Smith, 2018).

The EU may move on these issues, but the negotiations to date show more ground being ceded by the UK. The UK government has already abandoned its determination to be out of the EU Customs Union and Single Market by 2020. There remains an opportunity for the two negotiating positions to coalesce.

The alternative to finding a solution to the land border, even if temporary, is dire. Even if we ignore the security implications of reintroducing border controls, from a purely economic perspective a failure to reach an agreement would not simply mark a return to the pre-1973 border in trade terms; 'red tape', delays and costs will all be more extensive. These burdens will fall on businesses that have, in many cases for decades, been seamlessly building up supply chains between the UK and Ireland. Worse, uncertainty over the shape of any deal undermines forward planning by such businesses.[5] Reaching agreement on the trade aspects of the Northern Ireland land border is therefore essential to a workable Brexit. A trade agreement is not, however, sufficient to achieve this outcome. The focus upon trade to-date has distracted from the citizenship and rights implications of Brexit, despite the significance of these issues for Northern Ireland.

---

[5]   For many stories covering a wide variety of agri-food and industrial goods producers who are extremely worried about this prospect, see Tony Connelly's (2018) *Brexit and Ireland: The Dangers, the Opportunities, and the Inside Story of the Irish Response.*

FOUR

Citizenship

I'm not lost for I know where I am. But, however, where I am may be lost. (A.A. Milne, *Winnie-the-Pooh*, 1926)

Introduction

For some people, citizenship is little more than a logo on the front of a passport or a dropdown box on a form. It is possible to go through the whole of life without really thinking about what it means to be 'British' or 'Irish', let alone what it is to be a European Union (EU) citizen. Indeed, about 19% of Northern Ireland's population have no passport (The Northern Ireland Statistics and Research Agency, 2012, p 16). However, even within that group, many continue to attach symbolical importance to their national identity. For others, whose livelihood and residency depend on their status, rules around citizenship assume pressing practical significance.

Since the Brexit referendum, however, questions of citizenship have become more pressing for more people within Northern Ireland; there has been a growing realisation that different passports carry with them distinct benefits. When speaking about EU citizenship, derived from being a national of one of the EU's Member States, the most prominent of these advantages is the freedom to move and work across the EU. Post–Brexit, Irish citizenship will continue to confer EU citizenship rights, but UK citizenship will not. Calculations about the value of EU citizenship have moved many in Northern Ireland to apply for Irish citizenship, even when they would not previously have considered doing so. For some Unionists, such steps can be difficult to reconcile with personal identity; Ian Paisley Jr famously, and not entirely convincingly, sought to explain away an Irish passport as merely 'a European document with an Irish harp stuck on the front posing as a passport' (Rogers, 2016).

From flags to anthems and rituals to patron saints, national symbols are a pervasive feature of life in Northern Ireland, and Brexit increasingly intertwines aspects of citizenship and personal identity. The revival of the blue-covered UK passport is as much about nostalgia as it is an expression of separation from the EU. National identity – a nation's understanding of itself – underpins such changes. Think, for example, of the French national identity, developed around the revolutionary motto *liberté, égalité, fraternité*, or the devotion to the 'American dream' within the US. A sense of a distinctive national identity can provide a premise for independence movements (currently exemplified by Catalonia and Scotland). This is not a force to be trifled with; for all the talk of an increasingly interconnected world, the last century has been blighted by multiple bouts of destructive nationalism, not least the clashing national visions of Unionism and Nationalism in Northern Ireland (see Chapter Two).

The significance of citizenship in Northern Ireland

A core feature of the Northern Ireland peace process was a drive towards parity of esteem for personal identity choices, exemplified by the Good Friday Agreement (GFA) principle that it is the 'birthright of all the people of Northern Ireland to identify themselves and be accepted as Irish or British, or both' (GFA, 1998, section 2, para 1(vi)). It was not a new feature of the GFA that people born in Northern Ireland could choose to take a UK or Irish passport (or both); Ireland had explicitly extended its provision of its passports to Northern Ireland since the Irish Nationality and Citizenship Act 1956. However, in this provision, the Unionist parties that signed up to the GFA accepted that Ireland's passport law is not a threat to the integrity of the UK (Ryan, 2004, p 177). It affirms that individuals must have their choices of symbolism and identity respected, and secures equal practical rights for UK and Irish citizens (see Chapter Five).

This equality has been essential to the peace process. However, the GFA's approach to protecting the 'two communities' (the Nationalist and the Unionist) has neglected other groups living in Northern Ireland. The needs of those holding neither a UK nor an Irish passport have frequently been subordinated to the interests of balancing Unionist and Nationalist concerns (Crangle, 2018, p 36). The Roma and Traveller communities have, in particular, fallen between the cracks in a system of legal protections fixated upon citizenship (Northern Ireland Human Rights Commission, 2018). Brexit risks reinforcing this process.

Multiplying the categories of rights holder

In pre-Brexit Northern Ireland, EU passport holders have often been the objects of neglect, xenophobia and even violence: recorded racist crimes against EU nationals in Northern Ireland rose by 48% between 2012 and 2017 (PSNI, 2018, Table 2.6). Nonetheless, their legal rights have been guaranteed by shared EU rules. Non-EU nationals, on the other hand, are subject to a greatly different set of rules and rights. This means that there have been two main categories of rights holders before Brexit:

1. UK/Irish/EU citizens.
2. Non-EU citizens.

As a consequence of Brexit, these two categories will multiply. Not only will non-EU nationals receive different treatment in Northern Ireland, but there could be important distinctions between many more kinds of citizens. There will be additional complexities because of individuals' date of birth, residency and family relationships. If the terms of the December 2017 Joint Report are to be given legal form, two broad classes of rights holder within Northern Ireland could multiply into as many nine different categories:

1. Irish citizen.
2. UK citizen.
3. Dual Irish–UK citizen (who has no Northern Ireland connection).
4. Dual Irish–UK citizen (who is part of the 'people of Northern Ireland').
5. Non-UK citizen who is entitled to Irish citizenship (eg a Canadian citizen).
6. Non-Irish EU national (eg a Polish citizen).
7. Non-EU, non-UK national (eg a Jamaican citizen).
8. 'Worker' in Ireland with EU/UK citizenship (eg who works in Dublin and lives in Belfast).
9. 'Worker' in the UK with EU/UK citizenship (eg who works in Armagh and lives in Dundalk).

The all-important symbolism and practical consequences of citizenship are thrown into disarray by the creation of so many technical categories. The potential for administrative confusion is obvious, especially when people living side-by-side in Northern Ireland will have very different rights based on sometimes subtle differences that place them in one category or another. Residency, for example, is a significant complicating factor over and above the basic categories; the category of rights holder that applies to individuals will sometimes depend on where they are resident at the end of the Brexit transition period (currently the end of 2020, but with an extension on the cards). This is more complex than where one happens to be on a certain date; if an individual is usually resident in the UK but is abroad for work or a holiday on the day the transition ends, that would not affect their status. However, if an EU citizen takes up residence in the UK after Brexit, then their rights will likely be different from those of EU citizens resident before Brexit.

Everyday citizenship

For those who have the 'right' citizenship status, belonging to the group of rights holders who enjoy the broadest range of legal protections available in a country, the significance of citizenship can be frequently overlooked. One impact of EU citizenship has been to extend the number of people for whom these issues are not a pressing concern by reducing everyday differences between 'home' citizens and those able to say 'civus europeus sum' ('I am an EU citizen').[1] The same benefits, however, do not extend to Syrian refugees reaching the borders of EU Member States. Citizenship acts as a club, where the members get benefits and outsiders must pay a higher price for the same benefits or are entirely excluded. As outsiders to the EU club, Syrians have been subject to a morass of legal rules applicable to refugees, notwithstanding the conflict that they are fleeing (Trauner, 2016, pp 313–14). This same pattern occurs every day across the EU in less extreme situations. Non–EU and non–European Economic Area (EEA) citizens, be they from the Philippines, Egypt or Peru, enjoy fewer legal protections than EU citizens as a consequence of their status (Halleskov, 2005, p 181). UK citizens will soon find themselves outside the club.

---

[1] C-168/91 *Konstantinidis v Stadt Altensteig-Standesamt* [1993] ECR 1-1198, 1212 (AG Jacobs).

In the UK, non-EU migrants have long been subject to a particularly stringent immigration regime. A UK Home Office policy to establish a 'hostile environment' makes life difficult for migrants awaiting official decisions on their status, who lack the correct paperwork or who do not have a right to be in the UK to carry out everyday administrative tasks. The potential for this policy to go wrong was recently highlighted by the poor treatment of the Windrush Generation of Commonwealth Caribbean migrants to the UK. These individuals had a historic entitlement to live in the UK (some of them as UK citizens and some as Commonwealth citizens under the British Nationality Act 1948 reforms); however, few could show paper evidence of that entitlement many decades later. The hostile environment policy means that such individuals face regular checks at banks (Home Office, 2017a) and in tenancy applications (Bate and Bellis, 2017), can have their details passed to immigration enforcement if they witness a crime (Bloomer and Jeraj, 2017), incur high official fees (Home Office, 2017b),[2] attract an 'immigration health surcharge' (UK Government, no date),[3] and face the prospect of indefinite detention pending deportation if found – sometimes incorrectly – to be living in the UK illegally (Amnesty International, 2017).

These checks, often delegated to private and unqualified citizens such as landlords, impose considerable strain on all migrants, as well as people who *appear* to be migrants, and can hound people legitimately in the UK out of the country. The hostile environment can cause such anxiety that even those legally entitled to live in the UK avoid official channels for fear of deportation, detention or fees they cannot afford. Migrants are

---

[2] For example, in 2018, an application for Indefinite Leave to Remain costs £2,297 (per person), and an application for a two-year visa can cost £337 (per person).

[3] This surcharge amounts to £200 per year, per person (the charge is not applicable to those applying for Indefinite Leave to Remain).

thus often informally employed, rent homes on the black market and can avoid seeking health care or reporting crimes. This puts them at risk of abuse in employment (without protections like the minimum wage or workplace pension), trafficking and dangerous housing. It also produces wider societal impacts. Tackling crime becomes more difficult, rogue employers get away with undercutting the labour costs of legitimate businesses and public health issues can result from sizeable groups avoiding the health service.

The use of such administrative processes could extend to EU citizens following Brexit. The range of checks currently being discussed would amount to the hostile environment policy on steroids. Bodies such as schools, hospitals, employers, banks and landlords look set to be required to apply these checks across multiple categories of rights holder. There is significant potential for ordinary citizens obliged to conduct these highly bureaucratic immigration checks to get them wrong, to rely on their own prejudices or, indeed, to face punishment for not enforcing the rules stringently enough.

The likelihood of increased administrative checks stems from two UK government priorities. The first is the need to avoid a border between the UK and Ireland. Without checking who is crossing the border from Ireland, the UK cannot be sure who has entered the country by this route. Checks on people entering Ireland were discussed, but the idea was rejected because such checks would be patchy, would call for very high levels of cooperation from the Irish authorities and would need a greater harmonisation of Irish and UK immigration policy (UK Government, 2017a, paras 32–3). The second factor that shapes the push for further administrative checks is the desire to reduce immigration to the UK. There is no inherent need to monitor who is in the UK in such comprehensive and intrusive ways, and a different approach to immigration rules could monitor elements (eg employment) without checking so many aspects of an individual's life.

There will therefore be significant practical benefits for those who can circumvent the need for these checks. These include EU citizens resident in the UK before the end of the Brexit transition/implementation period (currently envisaged as December 2020), and Irish citizens in the UK (even if they take up residence or citizenship after Brexit). Such individuals will continue to hold their current social security rights, either under the plethora of UK laws that are part of the Common Travel Area or through the citizens' rights chapter of the negotiated Withdrawal Agreement. They will also have education rights, tax advantages, employment rights (Joint Report, 2017, para 31; UK–EU Joint Technical Note, 2017, row 19) and health-care rights (Joint Report, 2017, para 29; UK–EU Joint Technical Note, 2017, row 47). The right to equal treatment remains enforceable by such individuals in the UK courts after Brexit, prohibiting discrimination between UK and these EU citizens based on nationality (Joint Report, 2017, para 11).

The rights of those non-Irish EU citizens who become resident in the UK after the Brexit implementation period will, however, be as susceptible to restrictive immigration policies as non-EU citizens are today. Rather than being based in the Withdrawal Agreement, and therefore backed by the EU, their rights will depend on UK government policy. Ministers, in relation to the forthcoming Immigration Bill, have ruled out a points-based immigration system for EU nationals (BBC, 2016) and the UK and EU have stated that the movement of people is a shared aim for their post-Brexit relationship. These aspirations, however, guarantee little and there is nothing currently agreed that would prevent the UK government from applying its panoply of hostile environment measures to new EU migrants after the transition period.

Keeping the peace

Brexit's reshuffling of citizenship entitlements and rights could reshape community identities in Northern Ireland. The GFA describes Northern Ireland citizens' right to choose a UK or Irish citizenship as a 'birthright' (GFA, 1998, section 2, para 1(vi)). Although such identity choices have long been important to many individuals, there have been few practical implications of one's choice of citizenship. This is not to say that everything has been rosy for all since the GFA; complete parity of treatment has not been achieved. Among numerous (and often contentious) examples, shortcomings in social housing in North Belfast, recognised by United Nations experts, continue to disproportionately affect Catholic communities (Human Rights Council, 2014, para 73). However, these problems do not stem directly from the legal architecture around citizenship. The GFA's major organising principle, that British or Irish identity should not affect a person's opportunities, has held. Brexit threatens this position.

Post-Brexit, an individual's choice between the citizenships available to them will have practical consequences: Irish citizenship will also bring with it some of the benefits of EU citizenship. These choices will therefore not be primarily exercises in self-understanding. At best, the functional implications of citizenship choices will create split identities, in which individuals feel obliged to claim Irish citizenship for practical and administrative reasons, even if they self-identify as British. At worst, this change will see UK and Irish citizens living side-by-side with very different rights; a certain way to erode the consensus built around 'parity of esteem'. All of these post-Brexit effects are also landing in a Northern Ireland that has already been affected by Brexit campaigning itself, 'built on a narrative of Britishness' (Human Rights Consortium, 2018, p 10).

All sides in the negotiations have been clear that Irish citizens should not have their rights as EU citizens affected by the Brexit process. For those Irish citizens living in the Republic of Ireland, this is straightforward. However, Irish citizens in Northern Ireland will almost certainly enjoy particular protections in the final agreement between the UK and the EU. The EU Task Force's draft Withdrawal Agreement provides special recognition of the rights of Irish citizens who are part of the people of Northern Ireland (EU Task Force, 2018a, preamble). Protecting the rights of Irish/EU citizens in Northern Ireland, which will be territory outside of the EU following Brexit, will nonetheless be a particularly difficult task.

Many EU rights are only operational when inside of EU territory. Consider, for example, the position of Spanish citizens in Canada. They cannot use their rights as EU citizens to establish businesses in Canada with automatic access rights to the EU Single Market, as they could if they were based in an EU Member State. It is not clear what will happen with regard to businesses set up by Irish citizens in Northern Ireland after Brexit – the integrity of the Single Market implies that these rights could be lost. Nonetheless, as we saw in Chapter Three, the EU is pushing a solution in its draft Agreement that would see Northern Ireland treated as a separate regulatory area with special status, so it is conceivable that Irish citizens' establishment rights in Northern Ireland would be protected under such an arrangement. Irish Minister for Foreign Affairs Simon Coveney has termed this the 'Hong Kong' solution (Boffey, 2017).

Moreover, there are a range of personal rights that can and will apply to Irish citizens in Northern Ireland even when it becomes a non-EU territory. These include protections under the EU's Charter of Fundamental Rights (CFR), the principle of non-discrimination between EU nationals and UK nationals, and the ability to seamlessly travel throughout the EU and provide services in the other Member States. Such rights will not be held by everyone in Northern Ireland; they are EU citizenship rights, and thus conditional on Irish rather than UK citizenship.

Brexit therefore creates significant incentives for people to take Irish citizenship. As a result, some people will take Irish citizenship to access EU rights, even if doing so is at variance with their core identity. Indeed, the strain on the Irish passport service after the Brexit vote indicates that many in Northern Ireland and beyond are already taking this option (Peyton, 2016). This is a significant change in the Northern Ireland context. In the last census, only 1.7% of individuals responded that they had both a UK and an Irish passport (The Northern Ireland Statistics and Research Agency, 2012, p 16).

Those who do not take Irish citizenship, because they are unaware of its benefits or their eligibility to do so, or because of how they conceive of their own British identity, will enjoy fewer rights in post-Brexit Northern Ireland. These rights can manifest in quite concrete and material ways. EU law offers enhanced employment rights, for example, having driven forward equality and maternity rights (TUC, 2016). Such protections could, by contrast, be eroded in the UK post-Brexit (see Chapter Five). The ultimate Withdrawal Agreement between the UK and the EU will establish mechanisms to monitor and protect such rights for Irish citizens in Northern Ireland. These arrangements could leave two workers at the same Ballymena office with starkly different protections depending on their UK or Irish citizenship, threatening the idea of parity of esteem. After Brexit, the two communities will not be equally protected by law and only Irish citizenship will grant access to certain rights. This creates the potential for identity to once again become a highly divisive issue in Northern Ireland.

There are three possible responses to these disparities. The first is to try to ignore them and risk the build-up of resentment and the undermining of the current consensus. The second is to attempt to tackle them through ad hoc domestic laws, so that each time it becomes apparent that the non-Irish citizens of Northern Ireland are losing out, an amendment could be made in domestic law to equalise their rights. In this regard, embedding the EU's CFR in Northern Ireland's law is of particular importance. Although the CFR would be insufficient on its own (eg it would not allow non-Irish citizens of Northern Ireland to move freely across the EU), it would guarantee some of the most important rights to all (see Chapter Five). The third approach is a more formal, and much more satisfactory, route: the UK and EU could formally guarantee full EU citizenship rights to all of those born in Northern Ireland, whether they hold Irish citizenship or not. Only this approach fully addresses the problem of disparities in rights undermining the GFA's choice-of-citizenship provisions.

Beyond British/Irish

Northern Ireland is home to relatively few people who are not UK or Irish citizens. At the 2011 census only 3.37% of people reported having neither a UK nor an Irish passport (The Northern Ireland Statistics and Research Agency, 2012, p 16). Despite the small percentage, this amounts to over 60,000 individuals. Finding a place for these citizenships in post-Brexit Northern Ireland will be a challenge. As already outlined, such individuals will be at an increased risk of getting caught up in administrative checks of citizenship and entitlements. There will also be difficulties in agreeing the rights of non-British, non-Irish citizens relative to the 'two communities'. With the focus on developing equivalence between UK and Irish citizens, there is a risk that non-British, non-Irish citizens are disregarded or afforded only minimal protections.

This becomes all the more concerning when the details emerge. Under the proposed Withdrawal Agreement, for those EU citizens resident in the UK at the end of the transition period, their current rights will be maintained. This further isolates those individuals who either do not have EU citizenship or who become resident in the UK after the Brexit transition. There has been little attention to whether, 10, 20 or 30 years down the line, the UK authorities really want the task of distinguishing between the Irish people of Northern Ireland, 'other' Irish people resident in Northern Ireland, UK citizens, EU citizens who were in Northern Ireland before Brexit, EU citizens who arrived later, non-EU citizens and so forth.

Modes of citizenship protection

Brexit's likely creation of multiple different categories of rights holder in Northern Ireland therefore poses considerable challenges. Much of this complexity derives from how the outline Agreement between the UK and the EU seeks to protect different interest groups alongside legacy categories of rights holder. The Common Travel Area will continue, permitting UK and Irish citizens to move between the two countries and claim most social security benefits. Some EU citizens in Northern Ireland will continue to be afforded residual EU citizens' rights. These are rights that derive from EU citizenship, and that will be maintained for those EU citizens resident in the UK before the end of the transition phase. Another group known as 'frontier workers' – individuals who live on one side of a border and work on the other – are given special protections (especially tax simplifications). Anyone not protected by one of these specific arrangements, however, will have to rely on UK domestic law for their protections. These rights will be in the control of the UK government and Parliament, leaving such individuals in a more uncertain position.

Common Travel Area

The Common Travel Area across Ireland and the UK will continue to facilitate movement by Irish and UK citizens across these islands after Brexit (Joint Report, 2017, para 54). The outline Agreement between the UK and the EU allows for the continued operation of the Common Travel Area (Joint Report, 2017, para 47). The UK has noted that its Ireland Act 1949 will continue to apply to the interpretation of Irish citizens' rights after Brexit and that the Irish will not be subject to UK immigration law, though this could be subject to policy changes (UK Government, 2017a, para 22). The Act provides that Ireland is 'not a foreign country' and Irish citizens are not included as 'aliens' or 'foreigners' (*Ireland Act 1949*, section 2). In particular, the UK government has indicated that the Common Travel Area's arrangements will exempt Irish citizens from having to apply for settled status or a temporary residence permit in the UK (DExEU, 2018, para 6).

The Common Travel Area gives Irish citizens in England, Scotland and Wales an enhanced bundle of rights not available to other non-UK citizens. The rights provided under the Common Travel Area for Irish citizens in the UK (and vice versa) are not identical to EU rights, but substantial overlaps do exist, and the Common Travel Area is often more generous. For instance, the right to work without obtaining permission, to education, to health care and to social security are all covered by the Common Travel Area (UK Government, 2017b). The EU and UK have promised to continue to coordinate social security to ensure that these rights are obtainable (Joint Report, 2017, paras 28, 30). This is of particular relevance for Ireland, which must continue to grant any EU citizens living in the UK and then moving to Ireland the same social security coverage that a UK citizen in a comparable position would enjoy. In other words, EU rules prevent Ireland relying on the Common Travel Area to give UK citizens a better deal than EU citizens. The picture that emerges from the Common Travel Area is a positive one for Northern Ireland residents with Irish or UK citizenship.

For other EU citizens, possession of temporary residency will allow for the full suite of EU citizens' rights until that temporary residency is lost, for example, by losing one's status as a 'worker' (Council Directive 2004/38/EC, Article 7(3)). For most, this would lead to the individual being subject to the standard UK legislation on temporary residence permits or having their rights determined under the new category of settled status. Irish citizens are theoretically also subject to these rules, but they will possess the additional protections of the Common Travel Area even if UK immigration policy on temporary residency were to be tightened after Brexit. A note of caution is, however, necessary. The Common Travel Area is scattered across many domestic laws, treaties and informal understandings (see Chapter Two), and its provisions have become closely intertwined with EU law. It is therefore an uncertain and vulnerable framework on which to rely in its current state and desperately needs consolidation and to be placed on a solid international law footing (NIAC, 2018a, para 36). The Ireland Act could, moreover, be subject to change by the UK Parliament, for example, to require the registration of Irish citizens in the UK, without breaching the Withdrawal Agreement (Joint Report, 2017, paras 16–17).

EU rights

The citizens' rights agreement outlined between the EU and the UK is a significant milestone, setting out who will be able to have continued access to EU citizens' rights after Brexit and what those rights will be. The protections provided to those with 'citizens' rights' are wide-reaching. Eligible individuals will keep nearly all of their current EU citizens' rights as they are at the end of the transition period. This includes the right of EU citizens to be treated equally, regardless of their 'home' member state (Joint Report, 2017, para 11). Importantly, however, their rights will not evolve with new EU protections that emerge after Brexit, nor can these rights necessarily be transferred to another EU country (eg under current proposals, UK pensioners in Spain will retain their rights in Spain post-Brexit, but they would be extinguished if they subsequently move to France). Nonetheless, citizens' rights explicitly include the right to social security for workers, students, the self-employed and economically inactive citizens. Education rights, tax advantages, employment rights (Joint Report, 2017, para 31; UK–EU Joint Technical Note, 2017, row 19) and health-care rights (Joint Report, 2017, para 29; UK–EU Joint Technical Note, 2017, row 47) are maintained. The right to equal treatment set out in EU law is maintained (Joint Report, 2017, para 31; UK–EU Joint Technical Note, 2017, row 47) and discrimination in respect of UK and EU citizens based on nationality is explicitly prohibited (Joint Report, 2017, para 11).

EU citizens resident in the UK on Brexit day, and UK citizens resident in the EU on Brexit day, will be entitled to continuing citizens' rights. This residency requirement is critical. These rights will only be available for those resident on Brexit day. People seeking to relocate for the first time or return after their residency permissions have expired will not be entitled to residual EU citizens' rights. These rights are not afforded to all on an unlimited basis, but only for as long as an individual's residency continues to be valid. Valid residency for the purposes of the Joint Report and EU law can be either permanent or temporary. Those who already have permanent residency are entitled to have it converted free of charge to a document conferring citizens' rights (Joint Report, 2017, para 21). There is even an app to assist with the process (Colson, 2018). Those who do not already have recognised permanent residency are entitled to claim recognition on the basis of the Withdrawal Agreement if they have had five years of continuous residence as a worker, student or self-sufficient person (Joint Report, 2017, para 12; Council Directive 2004/38/EC, Articles 7, 16).

The continuity of this residence is not broken by absences of six months a year, or a single 12-month break for an important reason such as illness or pregnancy (Joint Report, 2017, para 25; Council Directive 2004/38/EC, Article 16(3)). In addition, a worker who reaches the state age of retirement as a resident is entitled to reside without having been resident for five years (Joint Report, 2017, para 21; Council Directive 2004/38/ EC, Article 17(1)a). So, too, is a worker who has two years' residency who stops work due to permanent incapacity (Joint Report, 2017, para 21; Council Directive 2004/38/EC, Article 17(1)b). The UK is calling these permanent residencies 'settled status'. Once acquired, this permanent residence is lost due to an absence of at least five years, otherwise permanent residents under the Withdrawal Agreement terms are entitled to citizens' rights for life.

Those EU or UK citizens resident for less than five years on Brexit day, and who are not otherwise entitled to permanent residency, will be granted temporary residence. As a mirror of the current EU citizenship rights, to stay longer than three months, residents will need to have worker status, be self-employed, be self-sufficient or be in education (Council Directive 2004/38/ EC, Article 7). If one of these statuses is maintained (and changes in status are permitted (Joint Report, 2017, para 20), then, it appears, temporary residency with citizens' rights can continue for up to five years before permanent residency is acquired (UK–EU Joint Technical Note, 2017, row 20).

For those resident prior to Brexit, the Joint Report also provides for temporary residence of up to three months with no work or self-sufficiency requirements placed upon them. However, in light of the two-year application window following Brexit day (plus the six-month grace period after that), this category is likely to be of limited relevance. Citizens' rights cease to apply for temporary residents when their residency ends, though there may be other rights afforded by national law. EU citizens in the UK and UK citizens in the EU on Brexit day without a legal right to be there will have no residual EU citizens' rights. National laws will take centre stage. The UK has not ruled out rejecting applications from those EU citizens in the UK (including Northern Ireland) prior to Brexit day who do not meet the requirements of even temporary residency (eg someone who has been unsuccessfully seeking work for some period of time and who has no means of supporting themselves). Those whose application is rejected will have until the end of the administrative/application period specified by the UK (at least two years) (Joint Report, 2017, para 17e) to secure residency status through another route or lose their rights to work and to access services.

EU law has allowed, and the Withdrawal Agreement will continue to allow, the UK to require EU residents who are not economically active or studying to hold comprehensive sickness insurance, and also allows them to apply 'a genuine and effective work test' to some (O'Brien et al, 2016, pp 15–18). The UK has claimed that it will do neither of those things in assessing settled status applications (UK Government, 2017c, para 11), but it has a track record of applying a version of this 'genuine and effective work' test to low-income EU citizens seeking to claim social security benefits (Department for Work and Pensions, 2014).

Citizens' rights will be equivalent to full EU citizenship rights when the UK departs from the EU but they will not evolve with any new EU law. This will create a disparity between two types of EU law: the rights frozen in time on exit day, and those that will evolve and are exercised across the EU. For those relying on the citizens' rights provisions that are available to EU citizens, these are locked down in several places. First, the whole agreement is framed by the provision that 'EU law concepts used in Withdrawal Agreement [will be] interpreted in line with case law of the Court of Justice of the European Union (CJEU) by the specified date' (Joint Report, 2017, para 9; see also UK–EU Joint Technical Note, 2017, row 1). An additional provision requires UK courts to pay due regard to 'relevant' decisions of the CJEU made after withdrawal (Joint Report, 2017, para 38). Relevant decisions are those providing clarification of pre-Brexit EU citizens' rights. Second, the Agreement notes that the rights that eligible citizens are entitled to are those contained in 'Articles 18, 21, 45 and 49 TFEU, Article 24 of Directive 2004/38/EC and Regulation (EU) No 492/2011' (Joint Report, 2017, para 31), but it does not make provision for similar directives or regulations passed in the future. Third, the draft agreement notes that citizens' provisions establish 'rights for citizens following on from those established in Union law during the UK's membership of the European Union' (Joint Report, 2017, para 38). This can be contrasted with the position taken in relation to future social security arrangements, on which the EU and UK will 'decide jointly on the incorporation of future amendments to those regulations in the Withdrawal Agreement' (Joint Report, 2017, para 30).

Within the UK, both of these legal positions will operate at the same time. EU citizens in the UK on Brexit day will enjoy the frozen benefits of their EU citizenship through the citizens' rights provisions (and will retain their full evolved EU citizenship for use when in the EU area). However, the provisions regarding Ireland and Northern Ireland (which are not otherwise contained within the citizens' rights section) guarantee that the people of Northern Ireland with Irish citizenship 'will continue to enjoy rights as EU citizens, including where they reside in Northern Ireland' (Joint Report, 2017, para 52). It continues that the Agreement is 'without prejudice to the rights, opportunities and identity that come with European Union citizenship' (Joint Report, 2017, para 52).

This provision is intended to ensure that Irish citizens in Northern Ireland will be entitled to the full range of evolving EU citizenship rights, and not have them frozen in time as a result of Brexit (see Chapter Five). This will, however, require that mechanisms be developed to ensure that the law in force in Northern Ireland, at least as far as the people of Northern Ireland with Irish citizenship are concerned, keeps pace – in perpetuity – with EU citizenship provisions. So far, little has been published on the nature of such post-Brexit arrangements. The terms agreed to date with regard to protections for EU citizens' rights post-Brexit are, however, restricted in nature and time-limited. For instance, under Article 151 of the draft Withdrawal Agreement, there looks set to be an eight-year deadline for CJEU oversight of citizens' rights, and other oversight mechanisms might also conclude at that point. There are not, at present, separate special arrangements to cover Northern Ireland's permanent population of EU citizens.

The final frontier (workers)

The rights of frontier workers are given special mention in the Phase 1 Report. Frontier workers live on one side of a border and work on another. They are defined within EU law as 'any person pursuing an activity as an employed or self-employed person in a Member State and who resides in another Member State to which he returns as a rule daily or at least once a week' (Council Directive 2004/38/EC, Article 1(f)). In 2001, estimates suggested that around 9,000 Northern Ireland residents were working in Ireland and 9,000 Irish residents were working in Northern Ireland (PricewaterhouseCoopers, 2001). As business has become increasingly integrated across the Irish border, these numbers have expanded to around 30,000 frontier workers crossing the Irish border daily (NIAC, 2018a, paras 5–7). On top of these figures, there are further Great Britain residents travelling to Ireland for work and vice versa.

This status will more generally apply to an individual living in the UK who is a 'worker' within another EU Member State and EU citizens living in a remaining EU Member State and working in the UK at the date of withdrawal. Frontier workers are defined under EU law and a Joint Technical Note as 'a UK national or an EU citizen pursuing genuine and effective work as an employed or self-employed person in one or more States and who resides in another State' (UK–EU Joint Technical Note, 2017, row 4a). Such people have their current rights to work and residence protected (UK–EU Joint Technical Note, 2017, rows

4, 4a). In the Irish context, this will require the UK to uphold the existing rights of EU citizen workers resident in the UK who work in Ireland, and the existing rights of EU citizen workers resident in Ireland who work in the UK. For example, someone who is a 'worker' in Cork at the date of Brexit and who lives in Belfast is protected (providing they have UK or EU citizenship). Ireland will have to protect their existing rights as a worker and the UK must protect their existing rights as a resident.

These requirements go beyond the 'Ireland and Northern Ireland' and the Common Travel Area commitments as they extend working rights to a wider number of individuals. Most Northern Ireland residents are entitled to dual UK–Irish citizenship and can maintain these rights through that route. Irish citizens are also entitled to 'ongoing' EU rights within Northern Ireland. However, there are certain categories of individual for whom the frontier worker classification is especially important, including those living and working in border communities without an Irish (or EU) citizenship entitlement. For example, as a result of the frontier workers provision, a UK citizen with no entitlement to EU citizenship will be able to continue living in Strabane in Northern Ireland and working across the border in Lifford with the same rights. These rights only remain for as long as the individual's frontier worker status is maintained. Therefore, any gaps in cross-border employment could cause some individuals to lose their right to work under EU terms except in some limited circumstances (UK–EU Joint Technical Note, 2017, row 4a). These include for reasons of illness, involuntary unemployment after a year or more employment, or the undertaking of vocational training (Council Directive 2004/38/EC, Articles 7(3)a, b, d).

Frontier workers, however, will only be entitled to a six-month cross-border employment gap where they are on a fixed-term contract of less than one year long or are involuntarily unemployed after less than a year of employment (Council Directive 2004/38/EC, Article 7(3)c). This potential for the loss of 'worker' status, and, with it, the ability to work on the other side of the border as a consequence of unemployment, will lead to increased precarity and fewer employment options for those living near the border. The point at which individuals are determined to be frontier workers is at the end of the transition period; those whose short-term contract ends or who are made involuntarily unemployed from short-term employment, at any point until six months before the end of the transition, are currently at risk of losing the right to work under EU terms.

This leaves a number of cross-border industries vulnerable. For businesses that rely on a turnover of EU workers, the impact will be especially acute. For those frontier workers who are in a settled pattern of cross-border working, rights will continue, and this will be critical for the small number of businesses who actually straddle the border. However, after the transition cut-off point, it will be much more difficult for businesses to attract new cross-border labour as individuals will be subject to many more personal checks, and increased barriers to living in two countries. This will have a disproportionate impact on border communities, which are likely to effectively lose access to a flexible EU workforce (Connelly, 2018a, p 44). It is possible that a bifurcation of the labour market on either side of the border will occur. Those with Irish citizenship will have an ongoing entitlement to employment rights on either side of the border (Joint Report, 2017, para 52), while UK citizens' access to employment on the Irish side of the border will be subject to the terms of the Withdrawal Agreement and the continuation of Common Travel Area terms.

Post-Brexit manoeuvring

EU citizens who arrive in the UK after Brexit day will be reliant upon the UK's domestic law. This is an unpredictable situation to be in. The UK can unilaterally and without much notice change policy. In the current anti-immigration climate, xenophobic clamouring can quickly seep into national law (as has occurred with the Windrush Generation).

The UK has yet to set specific conditions, but it has sought to reassure EU citizens in the UK that they are 'valued' and that the UK is one of the 'most tolerant ... places in the world' (Home Secretary, 2017, p 3). However, the UK government's June 2017 Policy Paper also noted that those EU citizens who arrive in the UK after Brexit 'should have no expectation of guaranteed settled status' (Rudd, 2017, p 4). Some anti-immigration rhetoric of the Brexit referendum and the emphasis on border control would suggest harsher conditions for EU citizens arriving in the UK after Brexit. The UK may impose different immigration terms upon different EU nationalities arriving. This might involve, for example, minimal immigration processes for Spanish citizens but much stricter processes for Polish citizens. There are dangers for Northern Ireland in general, and border communities in particular, that they will get caught up in a national immigration debate that ignores the impact of having a policy that only allows a majority of EU workers to go as far north as the Irish border.

The Withdrawal Agreement might yet establish a relationship between the UK and EU that restrains the UK from acting entirely on the basis of its domestic law, and that prevents it from differentiating between EU nationals. In any case, UK government action in this respect would be restrained by the need to maintain good relationships with other countries that UK nationals prize access to (eg imposing harsh immigration terms on Dutch citizens might be reciprocated by the Netherlands imposing harsh terms on UK citizens). It is also possible that UK policymakers could eventually be forced to recognise the economic and social necessity of inward EU migration and develop a more open policy.

Conclusion

Citizenship and identity are prized and sensitive propositions. Brexit negotiations reflect at least some of these sensitivities. However, this has led to a complex array of categories of status for Northern Ireland. A significant concession was to guarantee to Northern Ireland residents holding Irish passports, or entitled to them, to continue their EU citizenship and to exercise those rights as far as is practicable. This concession is a significant departure for the EU as residence within an EU country is normally a prerequisite to exercising most EU rights. The accommodation of the continuing Common Travel Area is also an important concession for Northern Ireland, the UK and Ireland.

At the time of writing, these citizenship guarantees are of various legal strengths. The rights for Irish and EU citizens must be implemented in the UK in an Act of Parliament that has constitutional status.[4] It would be preferable for the Common Travel Area to be placed in a treaty between the UK and Ireland, but for now, the Common Travel Area is legally informal, consisting of a series of reciprocal arrangements between the UK and Ireland, which are liable to change. Many (including EU nationals arriving in the UK after transition and non-EU nationals) will be reliant on the UK's domestic law for residence rights, which will not have the same protected status as EU citizens' rights and can be changed at the will of any UK government in the future.

This leaves two main concerns. First, although citizens' rights protections under the draft Agreement are appropriately robust, there are many who do not qualify or who will struggle to bring themselves within a category of rights holder with secure residency. This will leave non-Irish EU citizens in Northern Ireland (and the remainder of the UK) especially vulnerable

---

[4]   *Thoburn v Sunderland City Council* [2002] EWHC 195.

as they struggle to establish legal temporary residency before the end of the transition period. They will be under pressure to find employment or study by Brexit day (or at least during the implementation period) to avoid relying on rights afforded only by UK law. A second major concern is the overlap and disparities between categories of citizen. In the Northern Ireland context, this is likely to be highly divisive and could undermine the political consensus around 'parity of esteem' and the equal treatment of the two communities.

In sum, if the parties to the negotiations are serious about protecting the GFA, they must pay much more attention to what have been treated as 'technical details' on residence arrangements. Such 'technicalities' will have fundamental implications for Northern Ireland. In a sensitive context, decisions made now will shape the region's views of citizenship and identity in the long term. Yet, even with substantial changes to the proposed jumble of post-Brexit citizenship categories, one thing is clear: citizenship(s) will become much more central to everyday life in Northern Ireland.

FIVE

Justice and rights

The peace process was built on a shared vision of equal rights and equal respect on the island of Ireland, as framed by the Belfast (Good Friday) Agreement.... We are now seeking assurances from the UK and Irish Governments that no rights are diluted as a result of Brexit. (Emily Logan, Chief Commissioner of the Irish Human Rights and Equality Commission, 2018)

Introduction

Many commentators acknowledge that Brexit will have implications for trade and economics, as well as for citizenship and their ability to live in the European Union (EU). However, what does the EU and Brexit have to do with human rights protections? This chapter explains how Brexit will impact the intricate human rights protections in Northern Ireland. Human rights were a contentious part of Northern Ireland's governance even before Brexit. The Good Friday Agreement (GFA) provided a baseline of domestic human rights protections, drawn from the European Convention on Human Rights and put into operation through the Human Rights Act 1998 and Northern Ireland Act 1998 (NIA). The ambitions of the GFA were also greater, requiring the development of Northern Ireland-specific human rights and a – so far, unmet – requirement that a Northern Ireland Bill of Rights should be prepared. Finally, the GFA introduced rights to 'equivalence' and 'non-diminution' of rights across the island of Ireland. Equivalence means that rights across the island must largely be the same (though there are obviously some differences, such as marriage equality, which have been accepted as not breaching the GFA). Non-diminution requires that these rights must retain their current levels of protection and evolve positively in future. These two principles ensure the same general commitments to rights in both Northern Ireland and the Republic of Ireland, even if there are some local deviations.

Figure 3: The Brexit process and human rights

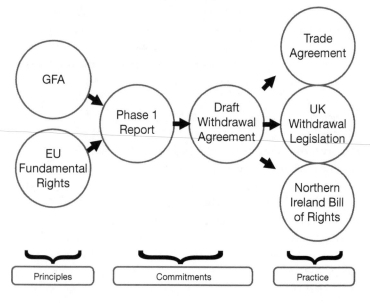

Beyond re-categorising the holders of certain rights (see Chapter Four), Brexit could radically alter the nature of human rights protections in Northern Ireland. This chapter addresses what Brexit means for human rights in terms of principles, commitments and practice (see Figure 3) – although some elements of those will inevitably remain fluid until Brexit negotiations end. First, we explain the principles laid down by the GFA and the EU's human rights architecture. Second, we evaluate how these principles have shaped the draft Withdrawal Agreement and its Protocol on Ireland/Northern Ireland. Third, we evaluate how these principles and commitments will shape any future agreement on the post-Brexit EU–UK relationship, the UK Parliament's withdrawal legislation and a potential Northern Ireland Bill of Rights.

Principles

The EU and human rights

The EU's significance for human rights in Northern Ireland, and the UK as a whole, was difficult to appreciate until the aftermath of the Brexit referendum, even for human rights experts. On a day-to-day basis, most human rights cases are brought under the Human Rights Act. This meant that despite the EU rights system always being there in the background and giving many of the same protections as the Human Rights Act, the cases that relied on EU rights tended to be in areas where the Human Rights Act was weaker. In the UK at least, the EU rights system has been most used in specific areas such as environmental law (Brennan et al, 2017) or data protection (De Hert and Papakonstantinou, 2017). The EU rights system has nonetheless had a considerable stabilising effect upon a wide range of rights that is only beginning to be appreciated. This system developed as part of the EU's efforts to make its organisational values explicit (see Table 1).

Table 1: Relevant aspects of the Treaty of the European Union, Articles 2 and 3

EU values	EU goals
Human Dignity	To promote peace, its values and the well-being of its citizens
Freedom	To offer freedom, security and justice without internal borders
Democracy	Sustainable development based on balanced economic growth and price stability, a highly competitive market economy with full employment and social progress, and environmental protection
Equality	To combat social exclusion and discrimination
Rule of Law	To enhance economic, social and territorial cohesion and solidarity among member countries
Human Rights	To respect the rich cultural and linguistic diversity of its citizens

Within the network of treaties, regulations, directives and Court of Justice of the European Union (CJEU) decisions that make up its legal system, the EU presents itself as an organisation that operates on the basis of human rights (which it calls 'fundamental rights'). Although, for the EU, rights were historically linked directly to participation in the Single Market, as the powers and responsibilities of the EU have expanded, so has the extent of the rights protected. The creation of the EU Charter of Fundamental Rights (CFR) in 2000 gave human rights further importance within EU law. The CFR complements the European Convention for the Protection of Human Rights (ECHR) (which has been around since 1950) and provides a sort of 'ECHR-plus' for the EU and its Member States. Although the ECHR and other international human rights treaties that the UK has signed duplicate many of these rights, others are specific to EU law. It is also especially important that the EU's legal system provides effective structures for enforcing rights (an area where many other human rights systems struggle). Also crucial is the way in which the CFR sets a tone for the development of policy in areas such as asylum, data protection, health care, social security, environmental protection and equality, where protections are developed and extended by EU law.

There is nothing in Northern Ireland's constitutional status or the GFA that requires the UK to be a member of the EU's human rights institutions or directly signed up to its standards. However, what *is* needed is equivalence with Ireland. After Brexit, that equivalence will need Northern Ireland to be closely aligned with the standards of the EU's human rights regime, as well as its various methods of enforcement. This is the basis on which the draft Withdrawal Agreement and Phase 1 Report are composed. Even after Brexit, therefore, EU human rights will remain relevant to Northern Ireland's human rights landscape.

The GFA's non-diminution and equivalence principles

The GFA's conclusion necessitated a major overhaul of Northern Ireland's human rights landscape. The GFA is binding under international law and is part of Irish Constitutional law. Following the Withdrawal Agreement, the GFA will likely become something that the CJEU will take into consideration when interpreting law, and the European Commission will similarly pay attention to it when proposing new law that touches upon Northern Ireland. However, the relationship between the GFA and Brexit has been hotly contested. The UK government has repeatedly pledged to honour its GFA obligations (Brokenshire, 2017) but has often been evasive when it comes to identifying the extent of those commitments, falling back on mantras like 'no one wants to see a return to the borders of the past' (May, 2017a, para 4.2). While such statements are intended to reassure, as no one really expects a return to a border patrolled by the military, promising that there will be no return to this past is a guarantee that fails to engage with reality.

The UK government has rejected efforts to put the GFA principles in domestic law following Brexit, saying that a raft of legislation has already fulfilled the UK's law-making obligations and that Brexit does not undermine these measures (Raab, 2017). However, the GFA has only partially been incorporated into the UK's domestic law. For some, the UK government's evasiveness is disconcerting when it comes to such a fundamental agreement. Lady Sylvia Hermon MP and Lord Patten have led efforts in Parliament to add a declaration on the GFA principles into the Brexit legislation. Their argument has been that the GFA 'has to be kept at all costs' (Patten, 2018).

Others, however, seek to portray the GFA as an irrelevance, coalescing around the claim of former First Minister David Trimble (2017) that '[i]t is not true that Brexit in any way threatens the peace process'. The Shadow Trade Secretary, Barry Gardiner, was forced to apologise after claiming it was little more than a 'shibboleth' (Allegretti, 2018). Recognising the risk that the GFA poses to their desired Brexit outcomes, leading Brexiteers, including Kate Hoey MP and Daniel Hannan MEP, have instead sought to portray the GFA as an outdated inconvenience that needs to be abandoned (NIAC, 2018b, Q302). These interventions either fail to appreciate the GFA's implications or actively seek to downplay them and mire them in doubt.

Certain parts of the GFA are, however, particularly difficult to wish away. The GFA and the later agreements, which mark milestones in the Northern Ireland peace process, are peppered with human rights commitments (Smith et al, 2016, pp 82–3). The GFA explicitly identifies human rights as sustaining Northern Ireland's democratic institutions, as a platform for building a harmonious society and as an important aspect of cooperation between Ireland and Northern Ireland. The GFA does not require the UK's or Ireland's membership of the EU, nor does it explicitly require the UK's adherence to rights provided under EU law. However, it does assume continued membership and, as we will show, its terms are more easily realised within the EU's common frameworks. The peace agreement requires the implementation of rights that go *beyond* the ECHR (sometimes known as 'ECHR-plus') and that speak to Northern Ireland's particular circumstances. Rights provided under EU law clearly deliver this ECHR-plus ambition.

The GFA also requires that Ireland, which had yet to build the ECHR into domestic law in 1998, to have at least an equivalent level of protection as Northern Ireland. The idea of imposing human rights obligations upon the Republic of Ireland emerged from misunderstandings during the peace process. The then Taoiseach, Albert Reynolds, misinterpreted Loyalist human rights proposals as demands upon the Republic rather than as a statement of rights to be enacted in Northern Ireland (Mallie and McKittrick, 1997, p 224). In the aftermath of the GFA, this requirement upon Ireland was presented as a Unionist victory: the ECHR was not exactly popular with the Ulster Unionist Party's rank-and-file, but at least Ireland was being obliged to take 'comparable' steps (Morgan, 2001, p 241). However, this part of the Agreement has a long-term impact because it links the two legal systems in Ireland; keeping the legal orders in line in rights terms prevents a barrier to the eventual unification of Ireland (Harvey, 2001, p 252). Only 20 years later did the consequences begin to unfold as the Conservative Party sought to alter the Human Rights Act and Brexit started being negotiated.

The extent of GFA commitments are not always easy to figure out. The Agreement can be interpreted as requiring equivalent North–South rights protections, and mandating the extension (and, by implication, non-diminution) of rights protections in Northern Ireland. Whether the Agreement *should* be interpreted in this way, however, is both a legal and political question. Equivalence has not, to date, been interpreted as requiring complete alignment (as seen by different arrangements on reproductive rights and equal marriage between Ireland and

Northern Ireland). The GFA is, moreover, a peace agreement as much as it is an international treaty, and many of its provisions rely upon 'constructive ambiguity'; they can be read and presented in different ways to different audiences (Bell and Cavanaugh, 1998, pp 1345–6). Brexit might not alter these commitments, but it does focus renewed attention on their scope given their capacity to shape the UK's withdrawal from the EU.

Commitments

UK–EU Phase 1 Report

It is important to reflect on the December 2017 Joint Report as it gives clear insight into the intentions of the UK and EU as they attempt to give legal form to their post-Brexit obligations. Paragraph 53 draws directly upon the GFA's rights provisions:

> The 1998 Agreement ... includes important provisions on Rights, Safeguards and Equality of Opportunity for which EU law and practice has provided a supporting framework in Northern Ireland and across the island of Ireland. The United Kingdom commits to ensuring that no diminution of rights is caused by its departure from the European Union, including in the area of protection against forms of discrimination enshrined in EU law.

This passage identifies several key connections between the GFA and Brexit: the EU's rights architecture; the need for a whole-island approach to rights; and the UK's commitments to both the non-diminution of rights upon Brexit and retaining the prohibitions upon discrimination currently found within EU law. These commitments could be fulfilled by law applicable specifically to Northern Ireland or to the entire of the UK. This paragraph should be read alongside the UK government's commitment to 'full alignment' if no other solutions will maintain an invisible border (see Chapter Three). That 'full alignment' commitment extends beyond trade to touch on this human rights paragraph of the Joint Report. Full alignment also covers key rights protected by EU law, including workers' and environmental rights, where their removal would impinge upon North–South cooperation, the all-island economy or the GFA.

Although these commitments do not need to be written into the UK withdrawal legislation under the terms of the Joint Report, they will become flashpoints after Brexit if the UK seeks to back away from its commitments. They make it necessary to retain EU law that touches upon these aspects of Northern Ireland law, and prevent such provisions from being subsequently repealed or marginalised. This backstop commitment remains in place no matter the outcome of the ongoing negotiations and this will restrict post-Brexit law-making by both the Westminster and devolved institutions, at least as far as Northern Ireland is concerned.

Draft Withdrawal Agreement: Protocol on Ireland/Northern Ireland

In its draft Withdrawal Agreement, the EU proposes a human rights framework to apply to Northern Ireland post-Brexit (EU Task Force, 2018a). Although negotiations over this text are ongoing, these proposals reflect the picture established by the UK and EU in their Joint Report. The draft legal text includes an annex which features provisions relevant to Ireland and Northern Ireland. This annex, the *Protocol on Ireland/Northern Ireland*, has a lengthy Preamble and lists several texts previously agreed or issued by the UK and the EU. All of these documents draw upon the common core provided by the GFA.

Treaty preambles are not legally binding under international law, though they can be used to decipher the purpose of treaties and therefore remain important tools of treaty interpretation (*Vienna Convention on the Law of Treaties 1969*, Article 31.2). The Preamble to the Ireland/Northern Ireland Protocol addresses seven overarching areas. First, it notes that the situation in Ireland is unique and Brexit presents specific challenges in the context of the peace process. Second, it states that the implementation of the GFA and later agreements is vital to sustaining the peace process. Third, reconciliation between communities and the normalisation of life within Northern Ireland is recognised as essential and requires that the GFA's 'institutional' arrangements be sustained. Fourth, Ireland's EU membership – and, by extension, its human rights commitments under EU law – must be respected. Fifth, Irish citizens in Northern Ireland 'will continue' to enjoy, exercise and have access to the rights, opportunities and benefits derived from their EU citizenship (see Chapter Four). Sixth, EU law will provide a 'rights, safeguards and equality framework' in Northern Ireland. Seventh, the Protocol can be replaced by a 'future agreement' between the EU and the UK, but this must address the unique circumstances on the island of Ireland and protect all of the GFA.

The draft Protocol confirms the UK's existing commitments under the GFA and demonstrate the concrete links between the GFA and EU law. Besides the UK's commitments, the EU also acknowledges its own commitments to Ireland, the UK and the Northern Ireland peace process. The Ireland Protocol's provision on rights, safeguards and equality of opportunity are directly related to the GFA and reaffirm the GFA's baseline requirement that the ECHR is part of Northern Ireland's law. This will mean that the UK will have to keep the Human Rights Act for Northern Ireland unless a Northern Ireland Bill of Rights can be passed that does the same job. The Protocol also clearly states that there must be no diminution of rights and that the UK must continue to facilitate the GFA's institutions. This is also important as it commits the UK to maintaining a range of monitoring and democratic bodies for Northern Ireland.

Beyond the Protocol on Ireland/Northern Ireland, there are other aspects of the draft Withdrawal Agreement that address human rights. Other than provisions relating to citizenship (see Chapter Four) Article 11 – which has been agreed between the

UK and EU – states that non-discrimination on the grounds of nationality is prohibited in the host state and the state of work for those EU citizens affected by Brexit. Article 33 – also agreed – requires that Member States and the UK undertake a publicity campaign about rights and obligations following Brexit. These provisions provide general protections covering all of the UK but will be practically useful to Irish and other EU citizens who live in Northern Ireland.

In summary, the Joint Report and the draft Withdrawal Agreement combined do not impose new human rights on the UK, but they do require that rights standards are consistent across Ireland. Post-Brexit Northern Ireland's human rights landscape ought to remain substantially the same, with changes only to increase rights rather than curtail their content. This commitment will bind the current UK government and its successors.

Non-diminution of rights

The draft Withdrawal Agreement makes a commitment to the non-diminution of rights in Article 1 of the Ireland Protocol. Non-diminution is sometimes described as non-retrogression or non-regression; however, while these are similar terms – also requiring a state to avoid backwards steps in human rights – it is important to be clear about non-diminution and the way it is used in the draft Withdrawal Agreement. The principle of non-retrogression is an established idea in international human rights law (Wills and Warwick, 2016), but it has not previously been used in EU human rights law. Critically, a non-diminution guarantee prohibits backwards steps, whereas non-retrogression permits them if they are justified according to set criteria. Following Brexit, it will be essential that this difference is recognised. These non-diminution clauses will require that the CFR and all of EU non-discrimination law remain in effect for Northern Ireland.

This guarantee is essential because the EU has been an important source of some human rights in Northern Ireland law: first, where the CFR goes further than other human rights in Northern Ireland; and, second, where the EU has agreed to international treaties that the UK has not. As described earlier, the UK tends to get much of its human rights protections from the ECHR. EU rights protections, however, extend beyond the ECHR in areas including marriage and family rights, education, asylum, data protection, health, social security, environmental rights, and protections against discrimination. Some of these rights come from the EU's CFR but many are also scattered across general EU law. No matter the source of the rights, the non-diminution guarantee is intended to protect them after Brexit.

The guarantee also covers some rights that are not rooted in EU law that Brexit stands to undermine. For example, the EU has signed up to a number of international treaties on behalf of its members. Legally, when the UK leaves the EU, it will no longer be signed up to these treaties, but it nonetheless is required by the non-diminution commitment to replace these rights. The treaties that the UK will have to replicate or sign up to include the Convention on the International Recovery of Child Support and Other Forms of Family Maintenance, and the Convention on Access to Information, Public Participation in Decision-Making and Access to Justice in Environmental Matters (the Aarhus Convention).

Both the draft Withdrawal Agreement and the Phase 1 Report are imprecise about the meaning of non-diminution, but it could come in two forms:

- Interpretation A – A *snapshot* at the end of the transition period.
- Interpretation B – The *ongoing* incorporation of additional rights.

The snapshot interpretation would freeze the rights available when the UK leaves the EU and ensure that there is no retreat from the standards as they exist at the end of the transition period. The ongoing-incorporation interpretation, by contrast, would mean that there will be no diminution of the human rights associated with being an EU member state into the future. This approach requires the UK to continually integrate new developments, adding new human rights instruments developed in the EU and making amendments to existing rights. Interpretation A requires the UK to protect only those EU human rights laws in force on the day of Brexit. Interpretation B would sign the UK up to protecting all of the human rights protections that the EU develops in the future, at least with regard to Northern Ireland.

Interpretation A, in practice, fails to protect against non-diminution. Increases in EU law rights protections would be enjoyed by those in Ireland and the rest of the EU but not by those in Northern Ireland. This outcome would potentially undermine the Joint Report guarantees for the 'people of Northern Ireland who are Irish citizens' that Brexit will be 'without prejudice to the rights, opportunities and identity that come with European Union citizenship' (Joint Report, 2017, para 52). It would be all-but unworkable to have different rights protections between *Irish citizens in Northern Ireland*, who would have full and continuing accrual of EU rights, and *UK citizens within Northern Ireland*, who, under Interpretation A, would only enjoy those EU rights in force on Brexit day (see Chapter Four). Interpretation A of the non-diminution provisions in the Joint Report and the draft Withdrawal Agreement would also undermine the GFA's requirements of equivalent rights protections in both parts of Ireland.

In summary, the non-diminution provisions of the outline Brexit deal try to keep the ties between the law in Northern Ireland and Ireland, as the GFA requires. This is tied to the aim of reducing the significance of the Irish border for rights protection. An interpretation of the non-diminution provisions based on a snapshot of rights in place on the day of Brexit would not satisfy this aim as this would freeze rights in Northern Ireland while rights in Irish law would continue to develop because of its connection to EU law. Only Interpretation B, requiring the ongoing adjustment of Northern Ireland's rights protections to keep pace with EU standards, secures this goal. This reading of the Joint Report highlights just how distinctive the legal framework affecting Northern Ireland is set to become after Brexit and is another example of the significant complexities that remain to be addressed in the agreements between the UK and the EU.

Enforcement and monitoring of human rights

The GFA demands specific arrangements for monitoring and enforcing its human rights standards. In terms of monitoring, the GFA underpins the work of the Northern Ireland Equality Commission and the Northern Ireland Human Rights Commission (NIHRC), and their equivalent in Ireland, the Human Rights and Equality Commission (IHREC). The NIHRC and the IHREC are given special powers to work together as a Joint Committee where rights issues have a cross-border element. In terms of enforcement, the GFA requires that individuals are able to challenge breaches of the ECHR, or the as-yet-unrealised Northern Ireland Bill of Rights, through domestic courts and also requires that the courts must have the power to strike down Northern Ireland Assembly legislation that breaches human rights laws.

At present, the rights protections under EU law are monitored by several EU institutions, including the Fundamental Rights Agency, the European Ombudsman, the European Data Protection Supervisor and, ultimately, the European Commission. They can be enforced by mechanisms such as the European Parliament petition procedure (*Treaty on the*

Functioning of the European Union, Article 227) and particularly by Commission enforcement action before the CJEU (*Treaty on the Functioning of the European Union*, Article 258). Brexit will see the UK withdraw from these institutions and mechanisms, which results in a loss of human rights enforcement. This potentially marks a diminution of rights in breach of the GFA. It also demonstrates a contradiction in the Joint Report and draft Withdrawal Agreement: both insist upon the non-diminution of rights protections and yet seemingly facilitate the diminution inherent in Brexit. To follow through on the non-diminution promise, a Northern Ireland-specific solution to Brexit must once more be found: the UK will be able to withdraw from the EU, but it will have to maintain alternate mechanisms for rights protection in Northern Ireland. In the negotiations to come the GFA will continue to condition the substance of Brexit.

Separate to the UK's non-diminution guarantee, it has undertaken to respect the rights, opportunities and identity of the people of Northern Ireland who are Irish citizens (see Chapter Four). This promise is significantly diminished if it excludes procedural rights or rights to complain to EU agencies and institutions. To respect the full range of EU rights that Irish citizens (as EU citizens) in Northern Ireland are to have, they must genuinely have the same rights and opportunities in Northern Ireland as they would within the EU. This needs EU institutions' continued monitoring of their enjoyment of rights in Northern Ireland and their ability to complain to EU agencies and institutions. Such arrangements are not directly addressed in the Joint Report or the draft Withdrawal Agreement. This might be because of the sensitivities around the 'red lines' set out by Theresa May's government. The EU negotiators might well see no need to emphasise the logical consequences of certain promises made in the Joint Report until Theresa May has been able to secure cabinet acceptance of the main terms of the deal.

From rhetoric to reality

If the relationship between Brexit and the GFA has been slow to come into focus in the UK's political debate, this is largely the product of the UK government's fudging of the issue. For much of 2017, Northern Ireland was addressed by Brexit ministers almost exclusively in terms of trade and maintaining the Common Travel Area: '[W]e are wholly committed to the Belfast agreement [GFA] and its successors. We will work with the Irish Government to maintain the common travel area on the island of Ireland and not return to the borders of the past' (Jones, 2018).

The GFA's role in this picture was limited, seen as relevant only to individuals' choice of citizenship and some scattered issues of cooperation between Ireland and Northern Ireland. A greater role for the GFA was repeatedly denied. There has been much talk of 'close cooperation' with Ireland over Brexit. However, when the Irish government presented their GFA concerns in mid-2017 (in line with their role as co-guarantors of the peace process), the UK government actively briefed the press and other EU governments that Leo Varadkar was an inexperienced Taoiseach looking to make his mark (Connelly, 2018a, p 350). All of this boosted Unionist narratives of a meddling Irish government seeking to subvert UK sovereignty over Northern Ireland. For Ian Paisley Jr, the GFA issue could be dismissed as little more than 'a made-up grievance by the Irish' that did not need to affect the shape of the UK's withdrawal legislation (Paisley, 2017).

The UK and EU's agreed position in the December 2017 Joint Report shows up such claims as misguided. As we discussed earlier, the GFA's equivalence and non-diminution provisions are not mere aspirations; they are shaping the Withdrawal Agreement proposals and the EU's plan for Brexit. The UK government has therefore, belatedly, been obliged to start engaging with the Joint Report's requirements during the passage of the Withdrawal legislation. The problem with moving from principles and concepts into hard law is that the UK government has adopted the mantra that 'nothing is agreed until everything is agreed' as a way of procrastinating over detailed legal arrangements (and keeping all of the disparate elements of its House of Commons majority on side). Ministers have not yet fully explained how the agreed principles on Northern Ireland will translate into practice. We therefore need to explore how the GFA's human rights principles are influencing the UK's Withdrawal legislation, and how the UK's negotiating position has repeatedly been overtaken by events.

Practice

Human rights and the future UK–EU relationship

This section evaluates options for protecting human rights after Brexit. Foremost among these are the UK government's plans for 'a new deep and special partnership between Britain and the European Union' (May, 2017b). This relationship would extend beyond a free trade agreement, with the deal extending into areas like security cooperation. With regard to Northern Ireland, this policy has even stretched to proposing that the EU continue to provide funding under its PEACE programme after Brexit (UK Government, 2017a, para 8). This begs the question of whether the UK government would be able to satisfy all of the GFA's requirements through such an arrangement.

The UK government has not been keen to recognise that a human rights provision is a standard feature of EU trade agreements (Bartels, 2013, p 297). The EU is, indeed, under treaty obligation to conduct its foreign policy with respect to the principles of 'democracy, the rule of law, the universality and indivisibility of human rights and fundamental freedoms, respect for human dignity, the principles of equality and solidarity' (*Treaty on European Union*, Article 21(1)). These elements of the EU's trade agreements have often received bad press, being regarded as means by which the EU pressurises developing countries. However, they are also present in the EU's dealings with advanced economies; the EU and Canada, for example, made reciprocal human rights commitments as part of the Preamble to the EU–Canada Comprehensive Economic and Trade Agreement (CETA).

For the EU, any comprehensive agreement will likely have to involve data protection, human rights and possibly workers' rights in order to minimise the potential that companies operating in the UK and trading with the EU under any Brexit agreement could use a lack of such safeguards to undercut their EU-based competitors. This could manifest itself in an eventual agreement as clauses tying the UK into particular elements of EU law, or even basing the trade deal on a requirement that the UK remain part of the ECHR system of rights protections. Ireland, as a co-guarantor of the human rights elements of the GFA, will likely push for the deal to be comprehensive in these regards. The UK's commitments with regard to Northern Ireland will have to be particularly far-reaching to match the level of protection that it has already guaranteed in the Joint Report. Of course, while negotiations remain stuck at the withdrawal stage, the UK government does not have to contemplate how much ground it will have to give to secure its cherished trade deal. We therefore need to consider the other arrangements that will need to be put in place to secure the GFA's rights and equality commitments.

Human rights and the UK's withdrawal legislation

The European Union (Withdrawal) Act 2018 (once called the 'Great Repeal Bill') is fundamental to Brexit. Its first function is as a piece of UK law that will delete ('repeal') the European Communities Act 1972, the link that makes EU law part of UK law, on the day the UK leaves the EU. The gaps which will this repeal will produce within the UK's legal arrangements post-Brexit are sizeable, and there is not enough time or capacity to develop the thousands of new domestic laws necessary to replace EU law ahead of the UK's withdrawal. Therefore, the Bill has a second function: to copy existing EU law into a form of 'retained' UK law (but calling it the 'Great Repeal and Retain Bill' would have been less catchy). The Bill enjoyed a relatively clear run through the House of Commons, with the Government managing to block amendments which attempted to keep the CFR or which sought to clarify its relationship with the GFA. These issues, however, returned to haunt the UK Government in protracted battles in the House of Lords through the spring of 2018, sapping time and legislative energy that Theresa May could little afford.

Figure 4: The separation of UK and EU law by the Withdrawal Bill

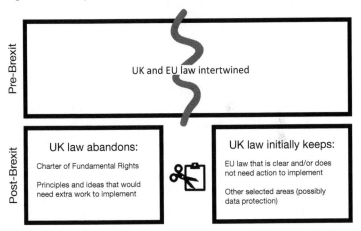

Generally, EU law rights that are recognised in UK law immediately prior to Brexit will continue in UK law after Brexit day. However, section 5 of the Withdrawal Act will remove the CFR from UK law. This means that the CFR's protections cannot be relied on post-Brexit to challenge new laws which would be harmful to the rights it contains. The UK government has downplayed concerns, insisting that 'it does not intend that the substantive rights protected in the Charter of Fundamental Rights will be weakened' (DExEU, 2017, p 4). The CFR, however, is the backbone for many rights, and removing it makes abolishing those protections easier. The CFR aside, under sections 2, 3 and 4 of the Withdrawal Act there will be many EU rights that are clear and/or do not need domestic implementing action that will remain part of UK law. These provisions provide a 'sticking plaster', maintaining rights equivalence in the short term. Under the Withdrawal Act, the UK Parliament will, following Brexit, be able to use the normal processes of UK law-making to change the EU laws that have been retained. Over time, this will mean that the UK will customise and remove retained EU laws and the country will move gradually further away from the EU model.

This approach to EU rights has the potential to create confusion. Take data protection as just one example. EU law's right to protection of personal data (*Charter of Fundamental Rights of the European Union*, Article 8) is more extensive than the rights found in other UK and European rights instruments. As the CJEU states: 'Article 8 of the Charter concerns a fundamental right which is distinct from that enshrined in Article 7 of the Charter and which has no equivalent in the ECHR'.[1] However, the right to protection of personal data is also part of the EU's General Data Protection Regulation (EU Parliament and Council Regulation 2016/679/EU, Article 1(2)), which the UK government has committed to retaining under the Withdrawal Act. On the one hand, the UK is cutting the right out and, on the other hand, is committing to keeping it. Are these data protection rights going, or are they staying?

Post-Brexit, the UK Parliament will be able to alter any retained EU law and thereby diminish such rights protections. The EU, conversely, could develop rights protections that

---

[1]   See C-203/15 and C-698/15 *Secretary of State for the Home Department v Watson* [2017] 2 CMLR 30, [129] (Grand Chamber, CJEU).

exceed its current baseline. Either of these developments would introduce divergences between the standards of rights protection in the law of Northern Ireland and Ireland. Such divergence is all the more likely in the context of calls for Brexit to result in less so-called EU red tape. For example, the 'red tape' klaxon is often sounded in relation to workplace rights and gender-equality protections, and even though the relevant EU law protections are initially retained through the Withdrawal Act, such complaints could pave the way for future divergence between the UK and Ireland.

Some rights – such as children's rights – will be culled much more swiftly. Children's rights are included within the EU treaties and the CFR. However, as they are not directly effective under EU law (because they set out ambitions, rather than clear, specific individual rights), they will not become part of 'retained EU law' under the Withdrawal Act.[2] By contrast, the right to equal pay for men and women doing equivalent work (*Treaty on the Functioning of the European Union*, Article 157) is directly effective and will become retained law, even though the equivalent CFR provision is not retained (*Charter of Fundamental Rights of the European Union*, Article 23). Although the CFR protections for asylum rights (*Charter of Fundamental Rights of the European Union*, Article 18) and victims' rights (*Charter of Fundamental Rights of the European Union*, Article 47) will not be kept, both have detailed EU directives, which mean they will initially be retained in the UK's law. These examples demonstrate just how complex the picture of "retained rights" will become after Brexit, making it difficult to track the UK's compliance with the GFA's commitment to rights equivalence.

---

[2]   Under EU law, for EU treaty obligations to have direct effect within Member State legal orders, they must be precise, clear, unconditional and not require additional implementing measures (see C-26/62 *Van Gend en Loos v Nederlandse Administratie der Belastingen* [1963] ECR 1).

Moreover, although the Withdrawal Act does an initial copy-and-paste job on substantial parts of EU law, Parliament has also given the UK government sweeping powers to make later edits to this retained law. Sections 8 of the Withdrawal Act grants ministers far-reaching authority to amend almost any legislation which ministers consider to have become in some respect faulty as a result of Brexit. These have been called 'Henry VIII powers' in a nod to the many-wived monarch's preference for ruling by proclamation. Under the terms of section 8(2), 'Regulations … may make any provision that could be made by an Act of Parliament'. In other words, ministers can change swathes of law with minimal involvement by Parliament, even if those changes involve amendments to statutes (and not just to existing regulations). In theory, measures such as the equal pay provisions enshrined in the Equality Act 2010 (and in the Sex Discrimination Order 1976 applicable to Northern Ireland) could be rapidly changed with limited scrutiny.

There are some restrictions upon these sweeping Henry VIII powers within section 8. They cannot be used to increase or introduce taxes, to change the law retroactively, to create new criminal offences or new public bodies. The powers, moreover, cannot be used to alter the Human Rights Act 1998 or the Northern Ireland Act 1998. These protections are significant, but do not fully protect the UK's GFA commitments against accidental or deliberate breach. In the course of convincing Lady Sylvia Hermon MP to withdraw an amendment seeking more clarity about the position of the GFA, the Brexit Minister, Robin Walker (2017), maintained that the UK government's 'commitment to the Belfast agreement is absolutely clear … [t]he Government absolutely support those principles, which are enshrined in the Northern Ireland Act, which is protected under the Bill'. However, the NIA is only one of the ways in which the UK's GFA commitments have been made part of domestic law, and some of these commitments are not covered by statute at all. The GFA therefore became a contested issue a$_g$ the passage of the Withdrawal Bill.

For many parliamentarians, led by Lord Patten and Lady$_{via}$ Hermon MP, protecting only the Human Rights Act and $_{l}$A against rapid change by statutory instrument did not sufficie$_{l_y}$ safeguard the GFA's broader principles (Patten, 2018). In t\ final stages of the legislative process the UK government made concessions to these concerns, introducing section 10 into the Withdrawal Act. This provision builds upon the NIA's protections by also requiring that ministers 'have due regard' to the terms of the December 2017 Joint Report. The implications of this turn of phrase might not be immediately clear, but if this provision is to mean anything, it must be treated as obliging the UK government to respect the commitments made to the GFA within the Joint Report when ministers use their powers under the Withdrawal Act. This amendment is therefore a specific fix; section 10 does not prevent future legislation being advanced by the UK government which conflicts with the GFA principles (even if they are affirmed in the Joint Report which this provision covers). It only prevents ministers from using their special powers under the Withdrawal Act to affect such changes by statutory instrument. Under this provision the Joint Report's principles play no larger role in UK domestic law. Further UK legislation will be needed to secure any final special provisions for Northern Ireland in any ultimate UK–EU deal (see Chapter 6).

The Withdrawal Act's removal of the CFR, and lack of safeguards around individual rights found in retained EU law, are significant. These developments mean that there is no effective legal safeguard in place to prevent a post-Brexit UK government from eroding rights protections, even if doing so would undermine the GFA's principle of equivalence. Suspicions around the Conservatives' intentions are fuelled by the party's attitude towards the Human Rights Act. Although this legislation is currently the main way in which the UK fulfils its human rights commitments under the GFA, the 2017

Co-ervative Manifesto gives notice of the party's intention to re-sider its operation after Brexit (Conservative Party, 2017, p). Since the 2017 election Conservative ministers have -intained that the UK government will 'further consider -ur human rights legal framework when the process of leaving the EU concludes and consult fully on proposals in the full knowledge of the new constitutional landscape' (Lee, 2017). This underscores the importance of looking at the position of human rights in Northern Ireland into the medium and long term. While there might not be an immediate issue with rights equivalence, the Withdrawal Act's terms risk the possibility of later diminution and potentially leave the door open to very different rights protections across the island of Ireland.

A Northern Ireland Bill of Rights

One way to buttress the commitment to the Joint Report in the UK's withdrawal legislation would be to revitalise discussions around a Northern Ireland Bill of Rights. The introduction of a comprehensive Northern Ireland Bill of Rights could resolve some – but not all – of the human rights issues post-Brexit. The UK government has said that it thinks imposing a Northern Ireland Bill of Rights in a top-down way from Westminster would breach the GFA (Bridges, 2016). Many Secretaries of State for Northern Ireland have insisted that any progress on a Northern Ireland Bill of Rights requires the Northern Ireland Assembly's consent (Villiers, 2013).

However, given the Phase 1 Report's recognition that special arrangements must be made for Northern Ireland, a Northern Ireland Bill of Rights offers a bespoke vehicle for addressing these requirements. The NIHRC's 2008 draft proposals on a Northern Ireland Bill of Rights should not simply be pulled off the shelf and dusted down, without thinking about the Brexit context. The non-diminution guarantee requires continuous integration of EU rights and full access to the remedies of EU institutions but as it stands, the 2008 draft of the Northern Ireland Bill of Rights would probably not meet these needs. As Ireland's rights protections evolve with the EU's, the Bill of Rights as it is would struggle to integrate changing standards. Revising the Bill of Rights in the context of Brexit would allow this new situation to be taken into account through a system of monitoring and updating law to keep pace with Ireland (Hermon, 2017).

There was some mention of the rights arrangements for Northern Ireland in the negotiations to restore devolution in early 2018, even if there was little detail beyond the recognition that the UK's withdrawal legislation could impact on rights in Northern Ireland and that there would need to be attention to Northern Ireland's 'particular circumstance' (*Draft Agreement Text*, 2018). However, these sentiments provide a launch pad from which to revisit the drafting of a Bill of Rights for Northern Ireland in the post-Brexit context. It may be the best option for ensuring non-diminution and equivalence on the island.

Cooperative justice arrangements

A love–hate relationship

The EU's cooperative justice arrangements showcase the UK's difficulties with EU membership and highlight another aspect of Brexit's human rights problems. The EU's arrangements for cooperating on justice and policing matters stress how far the organisation has expanded beyond its initial aim of establishing the Single Market. The UK has historically pushed for more extensive cooperative justice arrangements. In tussles that provided small-scale precursors to Brexit, however, Conservative ministers have increasingly sought to opt out from specific arrangements with which they take issue (Mitsilegas, 2016).

The CJEU's increased oversight of cooperative justice arrangements has been particularly problematic for the UK (House of Commons European Scrutiny Committee, 2013). The measures that the UK continues to apply, however, are seen by the UK government as vital elements of its post-Brexit relationship with the EU. In particular, the government is keen to retain the European Arrest Warrant (EAW) and policing cooperation.

Theresa May, when Home Secretary, argued that withdrawing from all EU justice and security measures 'would seriously harm the capability of our law enforcement agencies to keep the public safe' (May, 2014a), and during the Brexit referendum campaign, the soon-to-be Prime Minister explicitly highlighted cooperative justice arrangements as a major benefit of EU membership (May, 2016). The Joint Report between the UK and EU provides only a few details of the future of cooperation regarding crime or policing (Joint Report, 2017, para 92). Little of the EU's draft legal text of the Withdrawal Agreement touches on these issues. This is because, despite the continued importance that the Prime Minister has placed on security cooperation (May, 2018c), the UK government's insistence that Brexit will 'bring to an end' to the CJEU's jurisdiction regarding all elements of UK law (DExEU, 2017, para 2.3) makes continued justice cooperation much more difficult. The land border on the island of Ireland only heightens the importance of resolving this difficulty to ensure cooperation between the criminal justice systems of Ireland and Northern Ireland.

EAW

The EAW became operational in 2004, replacing traditional procedures used to transfer individuals facing criminal prosecution or prison sentences between justice systems.[3] The UK uses the EAW extensively, transferring roughly 1,000 individuals out of the UK under the EAW, and issuing over 200 of its own EAWs annually. With regard to Northern Ireland, the Police Service of Northern Ireland's (PSNI's) Chief Constable,

---

[3] EU Council Framework Decision, 2002/584/JHA, Article 1(1).

George Hamilton, told a House of Commons Committee that the arrest warrants 'are essential in tackling terrorism, organised and volume crime across the island of Ireland' (NIAC, 2016, Q162). The EAW process and the CJEU's protection of human rights in relation to the warrants have been subject to criticism. Some have argued that there are issues around fair hearing rights and that there is not a proper test to check whether issuing an EAW is a reasonable step (House of Commons European Scrutiny Committee, 2013, para 124). Nonetheless, the UK government has consistently emphasised the value of the EAW in protecting victims of crime (May, 2014b).

The operation of the EAW system is overseen by domestic courts, and since 2009, they can refer questions to the CJEU regarding the relevant EU law provisions (*Treaty on the Functioning of the European Union*, Article 267). A recent important court case indicates that the CJEU will apply the CFR to the operation of EAWs when it is deciding on the meaning of fair hearing rights, the right to liberty and the rights to private and family life.[4] Further, the EAW operates 'on the basis of the principle of mutual recognition'[5] and on the presumption that EU Member States maintain equivalent protections for defendants in their systems (*Extradition Act 2003 (UK)*, section 21). These two factors will make it difficult for the UK play a role in the EAW system if it does not maintain the standards of the CFR.

The UK's withdrawal legislation potentially undermines efforts to engage meaningfully with the EAW system. Section 6 of the European Union (Withdrawal) Act 2018 expressly prohibits UK courts from referring issues of the interpretation of EU law (in terms of those aspects which continue to apply to the UK) to the CJEU. The Joint Report in part reflects this stance – at least in the citizens' rights context – where the

---

[4] See C-399/11 *Melloni v Ministerio Fiscal* [2013] 2 CMLR 43, [54] (Grand Chamber, CJEU).

[5] EU Council Framework Decision 2002/584/JHA, Article 1(2).

jurisdiction of the CJEU over the UK will end after an eight-year transition period (Joint Report, 2017, para 38). CJEU oversight, however, is built into the EAW system, and without compromise over the CJEU's involvement there is no route to retaining the system which could be compatible with EU law. The UK government's express desire to maintain the EAW could therefore be frustrated by its resistance to aspects of the CJEU's jurisdiction and to the CFR's protections. The UK is sleepwalking away from the EAW system, and some individuals across the EU have noticed. They have used Brexit as a pretext to challenge their transfer to the UK under the EAW, arguing that the UK is not likely to protect their rights in an equivalent way in the medium term. In Ireland, Thomas O'Connor has argued that there was a real risk to his rights because of Brexit if he is transferred to the UK under the EAW system. In February 2018 the Irish Supreme Court referred the issue to the CJEU, effectively slowing down other EAW cases in the interim.[6]

One way to square the circle that currently exists on cooperative justice could be for the UK to follow Norway and Iceland. Neither country is an EU Member State, but both have concluded 'suspect surrender' agreements with the EU. These agreements create a similar arrangement to the EAW, though parties can still refuse to transfer their own citizens.[7] An alternative arrangement to the EAW that was negotiated sensitively could improve the rights protections for individuals within the system (House of Lords European Union Committee, 2016a, para 145). Critically, the Norway/Iceland arrangements do not come under the remit of the CJEU as disputes are sent to a meeting of governmental representatives. However, this dispute process only works on the assumption that few disputes will arise as the courts of Norway and Iceland will interpret the

---

[6] *Minister for Justice and Equality v O'Connor* [2018] IESC 3, [5.25] (Clarke CJ).

[7] EU Council Decision 2014/835/EU (27 November 2014), Article 6.

arrangements in line with legal developments before the CJEU.[8] Therefore, although the UK might escape the direct control of the CJEU, it would have to follow closely in the Court's wake as divergences would cause a breakdown in the system.

Any excitement over this avenue, however, needs to be tempered by reality: first, Norway and Iceland are in the Schengen free movement area, making these arrangements more straightforward than they would be for the UK; and, second, the agreements have taken *over a decade* to work up and are *still* not operational.

The old Council of Europe extradition system that pre-dated the EAW is not an option either.[9] Although these arrangements continue to cover some non-EU countries, other countries (including Ireland) have removed or altered their domestic legislation based on the old system following the establishment of the EAW.[10] This means that new legislation would be needed in the UK, and compliant legislation reintroduced in other European countries, to restart the Council of Europe system (House of Lords European Union Committee, 2016b, para 147).

Policing cooperation

Europol is the EU's police cooperation agency. Its primary function is to support the law enforcement authorities of EU Member States in tackling serious cross-border crime. Only EU Member States are entitled to full membership of Europol, though many other states enjoy strategic and operational partnerships. Some non-EU partners operate bureaux of law enforcement offices within Europol's headquarters. Such a partnership arrangement does not, however, substitute for full involvement in Europol (Campbell, L., 2017, p 4). It would,

---

[8]   EU Council Decision 2006/697/EC, Article 36 and 37.

[9]   *European Convention on Extradition* (13 December 1957).

[10] *European Arrest Warrant Act 2003 (Ireland)*, s 50.

much like the Norway/Iceland suspect surrender agreement, take time to conclude and be subject to the approval of the European Parliament. Historically, the UK government has wanted Europol to remain an intergovernmental tool for policing cooperation. It has resisted moves towards more integrated policing and autonomous capacity to tackle cross-border crime (Weyembergh, 2017). However, with Brexit removing the UK from the equation, it is likely that further integration of European policing will proceed speedily. This makes the UK's demands for inclusion from the outside seem all the more unlikely, with its demands for inclusion in Europol while having a series of opt-outs likely to receive a frosty reception from other members.

Local arrangements can supplement these EU policing arrangements in some respects. Prior to Brexit, the two-way relationship between law enforcement authorities on the island of Ireland was strengthened by a Joint Agency Task Force (Northern Ireland Executive, 2015). The Task Force consists of officers from the PSNI, An Garda Síochána, the Revenue Commissioners and HM Revenue and Customs, and enhances cooperation on specific areas of cross-border crime (Northern Ireland Executive, 2015, para 3.2). However, the operations of this Task Force will become a pressing problem post-Brexit as much of the legal basis for the sharing of information between police forces rests upon EU law. Post-Brexit, the PSNI and the Gardaí will likely have to devote more resources to cross-border crime, including smuggling and people trafficking. Should the legal movement of goods or people across the land border become more difficult, criminals will likely find it increasingly lucrative to develop ways to circumvent these restrictions (House of Lords European Union Committee, 2016a, para 150).

These cooperative justice arrangements have yet to receive much detailed attention from the UK government in the run-up to Brexit. Negotiation updates show that, at the time of writing, there is at best partial agreement on the draft

Withdrawal Agreement with respect to police and judicial cooperation during the Brexit transition period. That even less has been achieved on the future, post-Brexit relationship only emphasises how much of the legal landscape is still uncharted while discussions on trade policy drag on.

Conclusion

Northern Ireland is entwined in human rights provisions from international, EU and UK law. As Brexit looms, the difficulties of trying to wrench Northern Ireland from a complex landscape of human rights protections are becoming clearer. This complexity is not, however, an excuse for shortcuts that will have very real impacts on people's lives. As we have demonstrated, Brexit threatens the GFA's requirements for equivalence of rights in both parts of the island of Ireland and for the non-diminution of rights in Northern Ireland's law. It does this by eroding human rights protections based entirely or partially in EU law and by undermining the current mix of official human rights oversight bodies. It also cuts across Ireland and Northern Ireland's current cooperative justice arrangements, with no real sign of what will replace these (if anything).

In this chapter, we have explored the emergence of the principles of non-diminution and equivalence within the withdrawal negotiations. This appearance was not accidental, but drew on the GFA. These two key principles mark an effort to address some of the risks inherent in Brexit by preventing a gap opening between rights provisions applicable in Ireland and Northern Ireland. They could also spur a re-engagement with the Northern Ireland Bill of Rights project in order to produce human rights arrangements that address the needs of Northern Ireland's distinctive post-Brexit position. Such measures could offer real – if controversial – solutions to the human rights issues raised by Brexit (that is if politics surrounding Northern Ireland

and Brexit ever manages to move on from what 'full alignment' means for trade).

Many have disagreed about the degree to which the GFA justifies the path that negotiations are taking. However, for all the talk of a peace *process* in Northern Ireland, a peace agreement like the GFA exerts a powerful push towards the status quo. The peace process unfolds incrementally, and the overarching deal is implemented and tweaked as circumstances demand (for instance, changes brought about by agreements from St Andrews to Stormont House). However, the GFA is still the overarching agreement and is very much operative. This means that the tools of the GFA must work to counteract changes that would be an undue 'win' for one side or the other, or the conditions necessary for peace cannot hold. The inclusion of the GFA's non-diminution and equivalence requirements in the Brexit process is in part down to the strong bargaining position of the EU, but in any case, it is impossible to ignore such an important peace agreement in the midst of such huge upheaval.

SIX

Constitutional change

> I always maintained that our loyalties had an order – to
> Ulster, to Ireland, to the British Archipelago, to Europe;
> and that anyone who skipped a step or missed a link
> falsified the total. (John Hewitt, 1964)

Introduction

Brexit will not simply reshape the UK's relationship with the
European Union (EU); it will upset what the Belfast poet
John Hewitt understood as multiple interdependent layers of
governance and identity. In so doing, it could trigger wholesale
reform in the legal and political rules by which the UK and
Ireland are governed. This chapter examines these constitutional
implications and explores how these countries' constitutions are
shaping the negotiation and delivery of Brexit. We first examine
how a narrative of friction between the UK Constitution and
EU membership produced ideas of the UK 'taking back control'
through Brexit, and the ramifications of this mantra for the UK's
future relationship with the EU. We then assess how Brexit
impacts upon the 'territorial' aspects of the UK Constitution:

Figure 5: Nested governance in the pre-Brexit UK context

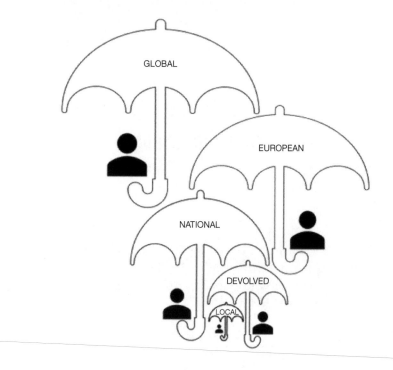

its devolution arrangements, and the shared rules holding the UK together. Finally, in relation to the UK, we consider how well the UK Constitution protects the terms of the Good Friday Agreement (GFA) that are threatened by Brexit.

We then examine the Irish Constitution and its relationship with Northern Ireland, particularly changes that have been made to the Irish Constitution by developments in Northern Ireland (including to the foundations of the state, citizenship and religion). These frequent adaptations to the Irish Constitution in light of Ireland's relationship with Northern Ireland open up the possibility of changes to electoral laws post Brexit giving Irish citizens in Northern Ireland the ability to vote in European elections. Another prospect is the passing of measures to reflect the possibility of the eventual unification of Ireland within the EU. This chapter closes with a review of mechanisms by which the GFA could be amended to facilitate certain aspects of Brexit, and what could happen if the UK sought to unilaterally alter or abandon its obligations.

Governance, disordered

Prior to Brexit, some theorists liked to imagine that a neat hierarchy of governance applied to territories within the EU (Ostrom, 1990, p 90). The constitutional orders of many EU states, and particularly larger ones like Germany and Spain, conform to this multi-level governance ideal, maintaining central, regional and local institutions. The EU operates over the top of these, providing a set of common rules that apply in areas in which the Member States have agreed to pool their powers (competences). Further EU harmonisation is driven by the promise that it is worth sacrificing some autonomy for the increased prosperity that cooperation brings across Member States (Della Sala, 2010, p 5).

Brexit pulls apart this orderly picture. The central feature of EU law is removed, to potentially be replaced by one or more two-way agreements on future EU–UK relations. Moreover, the relationship between national (Westminster) and devolved institutions (Northern Ireland Assembly, Welsh Assembly and Scottish Parliament) in the UK is unsettled. The big idea, in constitutional terms, is to restore the freedom of action of UK-based institutions, but this depends on an unrealistically rigid view of these governance layers, where higher layers always exert control over lower ones (Della Cananea, 2010, p 307).

Two parts of the UK (England and Wales) voted to leave the EU in June 2016, while the other two (Scotland and Northern Ireland) voted to remain. Against the backdrop of the Scottish independence referendum in 2014, and the weaknesses of power-sharing in Northern Ireland, Brexit increases the stresses upon the Union. These cracks will deepen further if Brexit does not deliver benefits across the UK. Without some sort of shared benefit, it will be very difficult to rebuild a national discussion; as one senior UK minister recognised, '[w]e could leave as a nation divided; a country split; an economy disjointed – struggling to forge a unified consensus' (Liddington, 2018).

Brexit will, at the very least, alter the UK's devolution arrangements. The first stage of this redefinition has involved clashes over whether powers coming back from EU institutions should go to the UK's central government or be transferred to devolved governments. This has involved arguments over transport, fisheries and agriculture powers (which have traditionally been devolved). The umbrella nature of EU law has meant that any internal borders (including within the UK) have been prohibited. However, with EU law being removed in the era of devolution, there is a real possibility that the UK's constituent parts could take different paths and disrupt the smoothness of the UK's own internal market. As Brexit looms, this means that brand new constitutional arrangements will be needed to cover areas that will soon become shared or mixed responsibilities between central and devolved governments.

Moreover, Brexit's constitutional upheavals do not stop at the UK's borders. If Northern Ireland is to keep facing towards the EU in some way, as suggested by the Joint Report, then constitutional thinking in the Republic of Ireland will also be affected. The most talked-about aspect of this is how the unification of Ireland as an EU member state could take place. The Preamble of the Protocol on Ireland/Northern Ireland makes specific reference to how Brexit sits within a domestic constitutional backdrop and the constitutional arrangements that have been made cross-border between Ireland and the UK. It underlines the need to respect, post-Brexit, Ireland's membership of the EU (which is written into Ireland's Constitution). The agreement by the UK and the EU also highlights the constitutional importance of the GFA, in particular, the principles of consent, power-sharing in Northern Ireland, North–South cooperation and the ability of the people of Northern Ireland to choose Irish or UK citizenship.

The UK Constitution

Hooked on a feeling: parliamentary sovereignty and Brexit

Much of the debate ahead of the 2016 Brexit referendum was framed in constitutional terms. Indeed, the Vote Leave slogan of 'Take Back Control' spoke directly to returning the EU's law-making competences and enforcement powers to UK institutions. The message was that EU membership undermined the UK Parliament's ability to make laws as it pleased, and instead gave the Court of Justice of the European Union (CJEU) the final say over the compatibility of UK law with EU law. In short, EU membership was presented as incompatible with the UK Constitution. This alleged misfit has continued to define the Brexit debate as Theresa May's government has sought to fulfil the promise of the Vote Leave slogan, despite rejecting the premise of the Vote Leave argument: 'Whilst Parliament has remained sovereign throughout our membership of the EU, it has not always felt like that' (May, 2017a, para 2.1).

The feeling that EU law is incompatible with the UK Constitution grew out of A.V. Dicey's influential 19th-century writings. Dicey presented Westminster as a sovereign Parliament, able to make or alter any law it chose through the ordinary process of passing a statute. This pure account of parliamentary sovereignty rejected the notion that any other body could challenge Parliament's laws (Dicey, 1885, pp 39–40). Leading Brexiteers such as Michael Gove have therefore insisted that for as long as the CJEU can rule that EU law is superior to UK statutes that conflict with it, this established account of the sovereign UK Parliament has been toppled (Wade, 1996, p 575).

In reality, this search for the feeling of sovereignty was always somewhat misguided. The UK's senior judiciary, schooled in Dicey's traditional approaches to the UK Constitution, took some time to accept that the law required them to 'disapply' UK statutes that conflict with European law. Long after other countries had recognised these obligations in full, European lawyers continued to fret about 'the delicate problem of Britain' (Weiler, 1990, p 19). This all changed with the *Factortame* case, in which the UK's courts finally acknowledged that 'it has always been clear' under the European Communities Act 1972 that enforceable rules of European law would have priority even over more recently passed conflicting domestic statutes.[1] The 'always' saved the Court's blushes over not having been previously clear on this crucial point.

The *Factortame* judgment was nonetheless grounded in the reality that the UK Parliament had authorised the UK to join the EU, and that its authority could always be restored if it revoked that authorisation. It still held the strings and, as such, there was no fundamental incompatibility between EU membership and the UK Constitution (Gordon, 2016, pp 341–2). After the Brexit referendum, the UK Supreme Court confirmed in *Miller* that EU law would only be a source of UK law for as long as the European Communities Act 1972 was operative, and that the UK Parliament had to authorise the process of leaving the EU.[2]

Concerns over the role of EU law nonetheless continue to dominate the UK government's thinking over Brexit. They are the motivation behind the following 'red line' in Theresa May's Lancaster House speech:

---

[1] *R v Secretary of State for Transport, ex parte Factortame (No. 2)* [1991] 1 AC 603, 659 (Lord Bridge).

[2] *R (Miller) v Secretary of State for Exiting the European Union* [2017] UKSC 5, [65], [121].

[W]e will take back control of our laws and bring an end to the jurisdiction of the European Court of Justice in Britain. Leaving the European Union will mean that our laws will be made in Westminster, Edinburgh, Cardiff and Belfast. And those laws will be interpreted by judges not in Luxembourg but in courts across this country. Because we will not have truly left the European Union if we are not in control of our own laws. (May, 2017c)

For a hard core of Brexiteers, these concerns would rule out the UK joining the European Economic Area or accepting the jurisdiction of the European Free Trade Association Court (on the basis that it usually follows rulings of the CJEU). This led David Davis (2017b) to downplay these options when he was Brexit Secretary.

These rows have a long and convoluted backstory. Euroscepticism within the Conservative Party was galvanised by the battles over the Maastricht Treaty in the early 1990s. For the Eurosceptics, the transformation of the European Economic Community (EEC) into the EU was a step too far, extending the reach of the European project beyond its proper goal of removing barriers to cross-border trade. Just a few decades later, many of the same politicians refuse to envisage continuing membership of much of the Single Market by exiting the EU into the European Economic Area, despite its more restrictive focus. This is despite the fact that the supposedly 'unimaginative' (May, 2017d) European Economic Area option would, at a stroke, address some of the most pressing issues of citizenship, cross-border trade and rights that Brexit creates for the island of Ireland (House of Commons Exiting the European Union Committee, 2018b, para 181).

The fantasy of control not only dominated the referendum debate, but has come to artificially constrain the shape of Brexit. It thrives on the assumption that a bilateral UK–EU free trade arrangement will allow much more control over domestic policymaking by UK institutions than alternative options such as European Economic Area membership would. This attraction towards free trade arrangements neglects the fact that such arrangements (when they eventually take shape) would be so central to the UK economy that they would, in fact, be extremely constraining on UK law and would be difficult to alter in practice. The difficulties in creating such an arrangement, not least in terms of reconciling it with the GFA's requirements, must ultimately prompt the question of just what is worth giving up for the feeling of sovereignty.

Devolution and the UK Constitution

The UK Constitution, unlike most others around the world, is famously not presented in a single document that is superior to other rules in its legal order. In this 'uncodified' Constitution, there are a number of conventions – political rules that regulate the relationships within and between public institutions. Although these conventions are not enforceable in courts, breaches of them can be described as *unconstitutional*.[3] Some of these constitutional conventions apply to the relationship between Westminster and the devolved legislatures in Scotland, Wales and Northern Ireland, and they could significantly complicate the process of Brexit.

These devolution conventions are relatively new elements within the UK Constitution. Between the 1920s and the early 1970s, the Westminster Parliament had a practice of not interfering when it came to matters that had been entrusted to the Northern Ireland Parliament. This practice was never elevated to the level of full constitutional convention. There was never any sense that the UK Parliament was prevented from making law for Northern Ireland (Calvert, 1968, pp 90–1). Devolution

---

[3]   *R (Miller) v Secretary of State for Exiting the European Union* [2017] UKSC 5, [148].

after 1998 was different. Lord Sewel, a minister responsible for getting the 1998 devolution legislation through Parliament, made a commitment during the process that was to stick. He promised that once devolution was operational, 'Westminster would not normally legislate with regard to devolved matters in Scotland without the consent of the Scottish Parliament' (Sewel, 1998). This promise (which became a constitutional convention) also covers Wales and Northern Ireland (Office of the Deputy Prime Minister, 2001, para 13) and has more recently been recognised in the Scotland Act 2016 and Wales Act 2017. When Westminster wishes to pass law in devolved areas, it asks for the permission of the assemblies, and consent is granted by the devolved legislature passing a Legislative Consent Motion.

This is the same for Northern Ireland (*Northern Ireland Assembly Standing Orders*, 2016, 42A, para 10). Westminster legislation that covers a 'devolution matter' needs a Legislative Consent Motion. There are two main categories of devolution matter: (1) a measure touching on a power that has been transferred to Northern Ireland's institutions (eg an attempt by Westminster to change health-care provision in Northern Ireland law); and (2) a measure that tries to alter the Assembly's powers (eg one which changes the Assembly's powers to make law concerning policing).[4] Therefore, in ordinary circumstances, because the UK Parliament's European Union (Withdrawal) Act 2018, Trade Bill and its proposed agriculture and fisheries legislation will all change aspects of the Assembly's powers, Lord Sewel's convention would trigger the need for a Legislative Consent Motion. With the additional complexities of the Assembly's power-sharing arrangements, such consent would undoubtedly require cross-community support (*Northern Ireland Act 1998 (UK)*, section 42).

---

[4] *R (Miller) v Secretary of State for Exiting the European Union* [2017] UKSC 5, [140].

The collapse of the Assembly in early 2017, however, undermines these constitutional safeguards for devolution. There is no functioning body to provide a Legislative Consent Motion, so the UK government can avoid this hurdle. While the Assembly is inoperative, the UK government has pledged to inform the Northern Ireland parties regarding withdrawal negotiations. In practice, however, this consultation has been uneven. Immediately before the Joint Report between the UK and the EU was concluded, the Democratic Unionist Party (DUP) enjoyed a virtual veto over the UK negotiating position on Ireland/Northern Ireland issues. This was a direct result of the confidence-and-supply agreement between the Conservative Party and the DUP at Westminster; the DUP were propping up a minority Conservative government. This close relationship calls into question the UK government's ability to deal with the parties in Northern Ireland equally, as is required by the GFA.

However, as uncomfortable as the Prime Minister's current position is, it is not without its benefits. Undoubtedly, the Conservative Party would rather it did not need to rely upon the DUP to govern. The government has also publicly insisted that it finds the collapse of the Assembly in Northern Ireland 'incredibly frustrating' (House of Commons European Scrutiny Committee, 2018, Q336). However, it still likely finds the current state of affairs preferable to the alternative of an operative Assembly. If the Assembly was functioning, the need for a Legislative Consent Motion would be undeniable and the Nationalist parties would, in all likelihood, have the votes to frustrate it.

In May 2018, the Scottish Parliament voted overwhelmingly to reject a Legislative Consent Motion for the withdrawal legislation, and a battle over its alternate legislation is set to be played out before the UK Supreme Court. Although the UK government will consider that the law remains stacked in its favour in light of the clause in the devolution legislation that confirms Westminster's sovereignty (*Scotland Act 1998*

(UK), section 28(7)), this struggle consumes considerable UK Government attention at a key stage in the Brexit process, and threatens to create an image of Scotland being bullied into Brexit. These factors enable the Scottish National Party, in office in the Scottish Parliament, to extract either concessions or profit electorally from the UK government's failure to compromise. For as long as its power-sharing institutions are broken, Northern Ireland is instead reliant upon backroom dealings between the UK government and the DUP.

Establishing rules for the UK's common market

In the early 20th century, borders as barriers to trade were largely thought of in terms of tariffs (see Chapter Three). Therefore, when Northern Ireland gained a measure of devolved governance under the terms of the Government of Ireland Act 1920, sections 21 and 22 prevented its institutions from exercising any authority over customs and excise duties. These measures were intended to 'secure uniformity' across the UK and were seen as essential to the functioning of the UK economy as a common market (Newark, 1954, p 552). However, as new borders went up across Europe with the collapse of old empires at the end of the First World War, things moved on from concerns about tariffs. Economists took increasing notice of a wider range of barriers to trade (Slobodian, 2018, p 42) and borders came to be seen as dividing up systems of regulation, not simply as places at which tariffs were applied.

An early acknowledgement of this issue came in the 1920 legislation, which prevented the Northern Ireland Parliament from enacting measures to affect trade 'with any place out of the part of Ireland within its jurisdiction' (*Government of Ireland Act 1920 (UK)*, section 4(7)). This awkwardly phrased restriction applied to measures adopted towards other countries, including Ireland, and to trade with other parts of the UK. It was an effort to stop the Northern Ireland Parliament from setting up its own set of regulatory arrangements to protect Northern Ireland's businesses against external competition. The efforts were, at best, only partially successful.

The 1930s were partly characterised by an old-fashioned trade war between the UK and Ireland, involving a tit-for-tat imposition of tariffs on each other's produce. The Northern Ireland Parliament joined in, opening up a more novel front in this skirmish through the introduction of special regulations governing the sale of milk (*Milk and Milk Products Act (NI)*, 1934). It was said that the purpose of the legislation was to protect public health, but its impact was really to shield Northern Ireland's farmers against external competition. Businesses from the Irish Free State, which were not entitled to licences to sell dairy products in Northern Ireland under the legislation, resorted to a legal challenge against the measures.

In *Gallagher v Lynn*, the UK's highest court accepted that this measure was not taken to restrain trade. It adopted a clearly hands-off approach to the legislation, accepting that since the 'pith and substance' of the enactment was a matter of public health, an area within the Northern Ireland Parliament's competence, it should not intervene simply because of incidental effects upon trade.[5] Indeed, the Court would only accept that a direct prohibition on trade would raise issues of compatibility with the 1920 Act. However, what the Court did not consider was that the terms of the legislation, requiring inspections by authorities within Northern Ireland, prevented the supply of milk by farms in other parts of the UK into the Northern Ireland market.

Perhaps the Court would have been more alive to this barrier had a less perishable commodity than milk been at issue, but the effect of this short judgment was to let the Northern Ireland Parliament away with it; the legislation 'seemed to run very near to protectionism in its effect, and it is hard to credit that this

---

[5] *Gallagher v Lynn* [1937] AC 863, 870 (Lord Atkin).

effect could not have been foreseen' (Calvert, 1968, pp 128–9). *Gallagher v Lynn* has nonetheless remained highly influential in the current era of devolution. In *Martin v Lord Advocate*, a majority in the UK Supreme Court endorsed the ongoing relevance of the 'pith and substance test'.[6] They did so, notably, over a vigorous dissent led by Lord Rodger,[7] who viewed this approach as overly generous to the devolved legislatures and not supported by the language of the devolution legislation.

The sudden denial of access for Donegal dairy farmers from their long-established market in Derry/Londonderry in the 1930s brings into focus some of the risks that borders can pose. It also shows the importance of 'regulatory alignment' post-Brexit and says much about the difficulties in maintaining a UK common market post-Brexit. When powers were devolved to institutions in Scotland, Wales and Northern Ireland in 1998, the boundaries of EU law were all expressly secured against adverse devolved legislation, including the rules of the European Single Market. After Brexit, a new legislative superstructure will be needed to prevent disruptive differences in regulation from appearing across the UK.

The UK government's solution to this issue is to return all EU oversight functions to central government through the European Union (Withdrawal) Act, and then later decide how to divide up these powers within the UK:

[S]ome powers are clearly related to the UK as a whole and will need to continue to apply in the same way across all four nations in order to protect consumers and businesses who buy and sell across the UK, in all parts of what we might call the United Kingdom's common market. That market is one of the fundamental expressions of the

---

[6] *Martin v Lord Advocate* [2010] UKSC 10, [13]-[15] (Lord Hope).

[7] *Martin v Lord Advocate* [2010] UKSC 10, [140].

constitutional integrity that underpins our existence as a
union. (Liddington, 2018)

The UK government, in other words, wants a window of
time to work out how a UK common market will function.
The Scottish government, however, regards this approach as
an insult to the devolution settlement. As we saw earlier, the
Scottish Parliament refused a Legislative Consent Motion for
the Withdrawal Act on the basis of this issue, and the Scottish
National Party (SNP) might well have the leverage to squeeze
concessions out of the UK government. Until the new rules
supporting a UK common market are devised, retained EU law
will, ironically, continue to provide the backbone of the UK
common market.

This can be illustrated by a more recent example of how
regulation can cause borders; this time, though, the drink
in question is a little harder than milk. When the Scottish
government introduced minimum pricing for alcohol, drinks
manufacturers launched a challenge on the basis of EU law
(*Treaty on the Functioning of the European Union*, Articles 34–36).
They argued that a measure supposedly adopted for health
purposes was actually a disguised restriction upon trade. The
UK Supreme Court recognised that the Scottish Parliament and
government put a greater weight upon 'combatting alcohol-
related mortality' than it did upon 'the benefits of free EU trade
and competition'.[8] The Court's conclusion was that it 'was a
judgment which it was for [the Scottish authorities] to make, and
their right to make it militates strongly against intrusive review by
a domestic court'. This outcome is entirely justifiable in this case,
but the Court's reasoning is still very hands off where devolved
legislatures are at issue. More active judicial engagement will

---

[8] *Scotch Whisky Association v Lord Advocate* [2017] UKSC 76, [63] (Lord
Mance).

be necessary in future cases if the UK common market is not to be undermined from the outset.

Constitutional instruments in an uncodified constitutional system

Brexit throws up another difficulty with the uncodified UK Constitution. Sometimes, it has appeared that the Constitution 'is no more and no less than what happens' (Griffith, 1979, p 19). This implies that all statutes are simply ordinary law and no law enjoys special protection. This creates a difficulty for laws that we regard as particularly important to running the UK. In other words, is it sensible to discuss the Northern Ireland Act 1998 (NIA), which was the foundation of much of Northern Ireland's devolution, as a 'constitutional statute'? Likewise, can we discuss the GFA as a 'constitutional treaty' in order to suggest that it has a meaningful special status within the UK's legal order? Moreover, once Brexit is done and dusted, what protections in domestic law will protect any special provisions put in place within the Brexit deal to cover Northern Ireland?

The NIA might have provided 'in effect a constitution' for Northern Ireland,[9] but the UK constitution does not give it any court-enforceable protections against ordinary processes of deletion and change. At best, if the courts do treat it as a constitutional statute, the NIA could be subject to special rules of interpretation.[10] This might involve judges refusing to allow its terms to be altered by words in a later statute that are not specific. However, this is a limited protection; it does not prevent the UK Parliament taking clear and direct steps to repeal the NIA or alter its terms (in the language of UK constitutional law, to effect an 'express' repeal). Under a 'pure' account of parliamentary sovereignty, then, even the principle of consent,

---

[9] *Robinson v Secretary of State for Northern Ireland* [2002] UKHL 32, [11] (Lord Bingham).

[10] *Thoburn v Sunderland City Council* [2002] EWHC 195, [60] (Laws LJ).

by which the people of Northern Ireland have to approve any change in its status as part of the UK (*Northern Ireland Act 1998 (UK)*, section 1), could be ignored by the Westminster Parliament if a majority of MPs insisted on doing so.

For some Brexiteers, the NIA provides the whole story when it comes to the UK's GFA commitments:

> [A]ll the substantive protections that were intended after 1998 to protect the Belfast agreement in Northern Ireland's domestic law were introduced either in the Northern Ireland Act, or in specific statutes that still apply or will apply in retained law as a consequence of this legislation. (Cox, 2017)

In short, for as long as the NIA remains on the statute books, the UK's GFA obligations have been fulfilled. The NIA is, however, a *partial* translation of the GFA's terms into domestic law. The principles of non-diminution and equivalence that can be extrapolated from the GFA are nowhere to be found in this statute (see Chapter Five). Under UK constitutional law, the NIA, at best, amounts to a 'constitutional' statute which reflects parts of a broader treaty. Senior UK judges have long sought to interpret legislation in a manner that is consistent with the UK's international obligations.[11] However, it should be possible, even within the terms of the UK's dualist Constitution (which separates out domestic and international law), for the courts to go further and to recognise that in certain circumstances, treaties, and not simply incorporating legislation, can carry constitutional significance.

Such a 'constitutional treaties' concept could apply directly to the GFA's special significance for Northern Ireland, and even to the terms of the final EU–UK Withdrawal Agreement (and, in

---

[11] *A v Secretary of State for the Home Department* [2004] UKHL 56, [27] (Lord Bingham).

particular, its Protocol on Ireland/Northern Ireland). Under this approach, the courts would have to accept that the GFA, and not parliamentary sovereignty, is the 'ultimate political fact' (Wade, 1955, p 188) of Northern Ireland's system of governance. If it is accepted that the GFA's terms provide the true foundations of this system, how could this proposition affect future litigation over Brexit? First, these issues have not been fully explored in any case to date. In the *Miller* case, the NIA and GFA were a bit of a 'sideshow' before the UK Supreme Court (McCrudden and Halberstam, 2017, p 343). The Court did not have to rule on their legal impact on the UK government's efforts to trigger Brexit because it had already concluded that Parliament would have to approve starting the withdrawal process.[12] Much remains that could be litigated. Second, it is arguable that Brexit does not *necessarily* undermine the GFA; it is just (very) difficult to accommodate within the GFA's terms. Therefore, nothing in the *Miller* judgment prevents a future challenge if the final Brexit terms do not make an adequate accommodation. For as long as the GFA remains in force, we would argue that the UK Courts should be receptive to challenges to Brexit developments that undercut its terms.

The UK government has repeatedly confirmed its commitment to the GFA as a whole. However, with some of its implications unclear (or subject to conflicting interpretations), and the stakes in Brexit so high, pressure could mount to not comply with certain GFA provisions. In such circumstances, the lack of safeguards provided by the UK's domestic law puts considerable emphasis on the good faith of the current and future UK governments when it comes to securing the UK's GFA obligations. Parliament can, however, play a key role in ensuring that the UK government sticks to its commitments. In the course of enacting the European Union (Withdrawal) Act

---

[12] *R (Miller) v Secretary of State for Exiting the European Union* [2017] UKSC 5, [129].

2018, parliamentarians have already obliged the UK government to limit the scope of ministerial powers to revise statutes post-Brexit in light of the UK's undertakings in the December 2017 Joint Report (see Chapter 5). If the Brexit negotiations produce a deal on Northern Ireland issues, the UK government will be expected to embody the key requirements of its Protocol on Ireland/Northern Ireland in domestic law. This will arguably require a statute which cannot be repealed for as long as any EU-UK deal remains in place (much as other laws which conflict with the European Communities Act 1972 will be disapplied by the courts, in line with the *Factortame* ruling, for as long as the UK remains in the EU). In other words, if any EU-UK deal is to be struck, Parliament is likely going to have to accept restrictions on its sovereignty where Northern Ireland is at issue.

This analysis assumes that UK domestic law will ultimately provide adequate protections for Northern Ireland's special constitutional status post Brexit. There are certainly considerable incentives to take such steps; if UK legislation does not provide adequate safeguards, any deal over the future of UK-EU relations will be jeopardised. Later in this chapter, however, we consider other routes to protecting the GFA under international law.

A border poll

A further constitutional concern raised by Brexit is the principle of consent. As discussed earlier, the idea that it is for the people of Northern Ireland to determine its constitutional status as part of the UK or part of a united Ireland is central to the GFA (GFA, section 2, para (1)(i)).[13] It proceeds to state that 'it would be wrong to make any change in the status of Northern Ireland save with the consent of a majority of its people' (GFA, section

---

[13] Agreement between the Government of the United Kingdom of Great Britain and Northern Ireland and the Government of Ireland (with annexes) (Belfast/ Good Friday Agreement) (1998) 2114 UNTS 473.

2, para (1)(iii)). As we have seen, this commitment is front-and-centre within the NIA, and its importance is reaffirmed in the context of the Brexit negotiations in the Phase 1 Report (Joint Report, 2017, para 44).

These commitments are ordinarily interpreted as applying to a 'border poll' on the status of Northern Ireland as part of the UK. Indeed, in the *Miller* case, the UK Supreme Court made short work of the argument that the GFA required the assent of the people of Northern Ireland to trigger Brexit: section 1 did not cover 'any other change in the constitutional status of Northern Ireland'.[14] This majority position is emphatic, but neither supported by reasoning nor necessary for the judgment. It could be arguable that should the constitutional status of Northern Ireland within the UK be significantly changed by any Brexit deal, for instance, establishing a Hong Kong-style 'special status' for Northern Ireland such as a customs territory separated from the remainder of the UK (see Chapter Three), then the principle of consent could arguably become operational. Control over economic affairs is a vital marker of sovereignty in international law.

These questions could therefore theoretically boomerang back to the UK Supreme Court once the Brexit deal is concluded, with less room for the judges to sidestep fundamental questions about Northern Ireland's constitutional arrangements, as they did in *Miller*. However, even if *Miller* indicates that such claims might be unfavourably received, there is a much greater chance that if Brexit goes awry for Northern Ireland, pressure for a border poll will grow. Theresa May is reported as not being confident of the Unionists winning such a poll if Brexit brought with it a hard border (Helm and Savage, 2018). Any question of such a border poll, moreover, also requires us to reflect upon

---

[14] *R (Miller) v Secretary of State for Exiting the European Union* [2017] UKSC 5, [135].

Ireland's Constitution, and the need for the people of Ireland to also consent to unification by referendum.

The Irish Constitution

Ireland, the UK and Northern Ireland

The 1937 Irish Constitution and its predecessor, the 1922 Free State Constitution, both set out the ways in which Ireland has dealt with Northern Ireland and the wider UK. The consequences of the 1921 Treaty, which ended the Irish War of Independence and created the Free State, and the evolution of both the UK and Irish constitutional infrastructures continue to have significance for Northern Ireland and are relevant to understanding the post-Brexit landscape.

The GFA led to a referendum in Ireland to replace Articles 2 and 3 of the Irish Constitution. New Articles 2 and 3 recognise the diversity of identities and traditions on the island and enshrine the principle of consent for any changes to the status of Northern Ireland. The amendment also requires consent in both Ireland and Northern Ireland for any move towards a united Ireland. Emerging directly from the GFA, the Irish Constitution distinguishes between the 'nation' and the 'state', though neither is expressly defined. Broadly, the nation is understood as the island as a whole, including Northern Ireland, while the state is the political unit, which excludes Northern Ireland. Some argue that the nation under the constitution could encompass Irish people living abroad (Forde and Leonard, 2013).

There were previous attempts at rewording these Articles. The 1967 Committee on the Constitution suggested alternative wording for Article 3.1: 'The Irish nation hereby proclaims its firm will that its territory be re-united in harmony and brotherly affection between all Irishmen' (Informal Committee on the Constitution, 1967, pp 5–6). Although it is unclear whether their harmonious vision included sisterly affection(!), it is interesting to consider whether brotherly affection in this context would be much different to, or extend beyond, the principle of consent currently in the Constitution.

Under Article 5 of the Sunningdale Agreement, which was a first and ultimately failed attempt at a peace settlement in Northern Ireland in 1973, the Irish government accepted that any change of status for Northern Ireland would require a majority decision of the population. However, this guarantee was lessened by the decision in *Boland v An Taoiseach*,[15] where the Supreme Court stated that Article 5 of Sunningdale did not negate the claim to sovereignty over the Northern Ireland territory claimed under the original terms of Articles 2 and 3 (Dorr, 2017, chs 13 and 19). In the wake of the *Boland* case, a clear statement regarding the meaning of consent was necessary (O'Duffy, 1999). This influenced the decision to align the words of the new Articles 2 and 3 with the terms of the GFA. These provisions of the Irish Constitution expressly affirm that a referendum will be needed in both Ireland and Northern Ireland to authorise unification:

Article 2

It is the entitlement and birthright of every person born in the island of Ireland, which includes its islands and seas, to be part of the Irish nation. That is also the entitlement of all persons otherwise qualified in accordance with law to be citizens of Ireland. Furthermore, the Irish nation cherishes its special affinity with people of Irish ancestry living abroad who share its cultural identity and heritage.

Article 3

1. It is the firm will of the Irish nation, in harmony and friendship, to unite all the people who share the territory

---

[15]   *Boland v An Taoiseach* [1974] IR 338.

of the island of Ireland, in all the diversity of their identities and traditions, recognising that a united Ireland shall be brought about only by peaceful means with the consent of a majority of the people, democratically expressed, in both jurisdictions in the island. Until then, the laws enacted by the Parliament established by this constitution shall have the like area and extent of application as the laws enacted by the Parliament that existed immediately before the coming into operation of this constitution.

2. Institutions with executive powers and functions that are shared between those jurisdictions may be established by their respective responsible authorities for stated purposes and may exercise powers and functions in respect of all or any part of the island.

Article 3.2 sets the basis for existing cross-border bodies that make decisions relevant to the entire island. This was essential in the creation of bodies in the areas of tourism, energy or health care, and may again become important to any new institutions that are set up post-Brexit.

Earlier, we discussed how the UK Constitution affords few protections to some of the fundamental aspects of the governance order (such as the GFA, devolution and EU law). The Irish Constitution is more proactive. The 1998 referendum, in addition to amending Articles 2 and 3, also introduced Article 29.7, which gives the GFA constitutional status in Ireland. Article 29 is the same provision that contains Ireland's commitments to the EU and its other international obligations:

Article 29.7

1° The State may consent to be bound by the British–Irish [Good Friday] Agreement done at Belfast on the 10th day of April, 1998, hereinafter called the Agreement.

The GFA referendum also introduced Article 29.8, which enables the Irish state to extend citizenship beyond Ireland, as well as other extraterritorial rights, including potentially voting.

The relationship between the UK and Ireland has influenced other parts of Ireland's Constitution in more subtle ways. For instance, a 1996 Constitutional Review Group noted that Article 44 contains provisions directly related to historical constitutional settlements between Ireland and Britain. The non-endowment clause in Article 44.2.2° and the non-discrimination clause in Article 44.2.3° find their basis in Article 8 of the Free State Constitution, Article 16 of the 1921 Anglo-Irish Treaty, the Government of Ireland Act 1920 and the Government of Ireland Bills of 1886 and 1893 (*Constitutional Review Group*, 1996). Further, the Intermediate Education (Ireland) Act 1878 and the 1831 'Stanley letter' are directly related to Articles 44.2.4°– 6°, which are the basis of the Irish education system. In contrast, Article 44.1 (respect for religion), Article 44.2.1° (freedom of conscience and free practice of religion) and the repealed provision Article 44.1.3° (the special position of the Catholic Church and recognition of the other Churches) emerged in the deliberations on the 1937 Constitution.

Referendums to remove or replace sections of the 1937 Constitution in reaction to developments in Northern Ireland pre-date the GFA. For example, Articles 44.1.2°– 3°, whose original aim was to contrast Ireland with the UK, also recognised the importance of the Protestant minority so as to remove any suggestion of discrimination in the new Irish state. Article 44.1 noted the special place of the Catholic Church while also recognising the Church of Ireland, the Presbyterian, Methodist and Quaker congregations, and Jewish congregations (critical in 1937) as existing. This provision was repealed in 1972 by the Fifth Amendment to the Constitution, by a vote of 84% (Department of Housing, Planning, Community and Local Government, 2016), in a move partly conceived as an olive branch towards Protestants in Northern Ireland (Daly, 2012).

As the 1967 Constitutional Review Group stated, these sections were:

> a useful weapon in the hands of those who are anxious to emphasise the differences between North and South ... [t]he deletion of this provision would, in particular, dispel any doubts and suspicions which may linger in the minds of non-Catholics, North and South of the Border, and remove an unnecessary source of mischievous and specious criticism. (Informal Committee on the Constitution, 1967)

Today, the Preamble and Article 44.1 are the only sections of the Constitution that invoke a specific Christian and natural rights basis to the Irish state.[16] The 1996 Constitutional Review Group recommended that the Preamble be replaced with a simple statement or wording that removed religious references in order to reflect the modern Irish state. The latter option included a section recognising the diverse origins and traditions, ethnic, historical, political and spiritual, their varying social and cultural heritages, and the sacrifices and sufferings, as well as the achievements, of the people's forebears, and that any aspirations to unity should be achieved peacefully through reconciliation and consent (*Constitutional Review Group*, 1996). Currently, there are no plans to alter the Preamble, albeit that Article 3 now recognises some of the sentiments suggested by the Constitutional Review Group in 1996.

---

[16] *McGee v Attorney General* [1974] IR 284, *The State (Healy) v Donoghue* [1976] IR 325, *King v Attorney General* [1981] IR 233, *Norris v Attorney General* [1984] IR 36, and *Attorney General v X* [1992] 1 IR 1.

Voting rights post-Brexit

In Ireland, voting law is a mix of constitutional and statutory regulation, which, at the moment, limits voting to those resident and present in the state at the time of the vote. This excludes those in Northern Ireland with Irish passports. The franchise for the election of members of Dáil Eireann under Article 16.1.2° includes '(i) all citizens and (ii) others in the State as determined by Law who are 18 and above'. This provision is also followed for local and presidential elections. Elections to the European Parliament are not covered by the Constitution except through the EU law adopted by it. Article 39 and 40 of the EU Charter of Fundamental Rights outline the voting rights of all EU citizens:

Article 39

1. Every citizen of the Union has the right to vote and to stand as a candidate at elections to the European Parliament in the Member State in which he or she resides, under the same conditions as nationals of that State.

2. Members of the European Parliament shall be elected by direct universal suffrage in a free and secret ballot.

Article 40

Every citizen of the Union has the right to vote and to stand as a candidate at municipal elections in the Member State in which he or she resides under the same conditions as nationals of that State.

Article 22(2) of the Treaty on the Functioning of the European Union furthermore states that:

[E]very citizen of the Union residing in a Member State
of which he is not a national shall have the right to vote
and to stand as a candidate in elections to the European
Parliament in the Member State in which he resides.[17]

These Articles establish voting and democratic rights as central to
the EU's understanding of itself and ensure that this is the same
throughout Member States. Beyond these common standards,
each EU state adopts its own arrangements, creating differences
across the EU. For instance, only five states (including the UK
and Ireland) have broken their states into multiple constituencies.
Denmark and Italy grant a right to vote for European elections
for some non-resident nationals living in third countries.
Currently, Ireland has one of the most restrictive arrangements
(alongside Bulgaria and Slovakia) in confining votes to EU
citizens who are domiciled in Ireland. Each state imposes its
own rules on who can be a candidate, but these must comply
with non-discrimination, minimum age and EU citizenship
requirements (the UK currently enjoys an exception for some
Commonwealth citizens) (European Parliament, 2018).

As the Oireachtas Committee on EU Affairs stated, Ireland is
among a minority of states that does not extend the right to vote
to its citizens abroad and the severity of that restriction could be
subject to challenge at the CJEU (Joint Committee on European
Union Affairs, 2014). The Oireachtas Committee recommended
that the Irish government should accept the principle that voting
rights in EU elections should be extended to Irish citizens
abroad. The Committee recognised that this would require
Ireland to define citizenship more clearly. Following the use
of 'people of Northern Ireland' as a category of importance
during the Brexit process, this need for clarity is heightened.
The recent Irish Constitutional Convention recommended
the extension of the vote in presidential elections to citizens

---

[17] See also EU Council Directive 93/109/EC.

living abroad, and, as a result, the government plans to hold a referendum on that question in the coming years. This process may provide a trigger for Ireland to re-examine all of its voting rules, including those for the European Parliament. However, it is important to note that the requirement of being 'in the state', which prevents many of the diaspora voting in Dáil, local and presidential elections before a constitutional amendment, does not apply to EU parliamentary elections. Changes to Ireland's voting rules for the European Parliament could take account of the Brexit process through ordinary legislation.

The European Parliament Elections Acts 1997 to 2013 cover voting in Ireland for MEPs. Under sections 6 and 8 of the European Parliament Elections Act 1997, to be on the register, one has to be a national of an EU Member State, Ireland or, currently, the UK. Post-Brexit this statute will need to be revised to exclude the specific references to UK citizens (unless they also hold the citizenship of an EU Member State). It would appear that it would be open to Ireland to grant the right to vote to Irish citizens outside of Ireland in EU elections without the need to change the Irish Constitution or EU law. It would only require Ireland to amend its European Parliament Elections Acts. While the case is strongest for an extension of EU voting rights to Irish citizens in Northern Ireland, such a change could cover all Irish citizens living in any part of the UK.

Citizenship and the benefits that come with it are about to become a critical part of the post-Brexit landscape in Northern Ireland. The idea of Irish citizenship originated in Article 3 of the Constitution of the Irish Free State, and whoever had citizenship in the Free State carried this entitlement over to the 1937 Constitution. Under the Irish Free State Constitution, individuals are citizens if they: (a) had been living within the Irish Free State and born in Ireland; (b) had a parent who was born in Ireland; or (c) had been 'ordinarily resident' in the 'area of the jurisdiction' of the Irish Free State for at least seven years. The Constitution's reference to the 'jurisdiction' of the

Free State was interpreted to mean the entire island (*Articles of Agreement for a Treaty between Great Britain and Ireland 1921*, Articles 11–12). This caused its own controversy and meant that the Northern Ireland Parliament gave notice to London and Dublin that it did not wish to come under the jurisdiction of the Free State (*Parliamentary Papers of Northern Ireland*, 1922, pp 191–2). It did this on 13 December 1922, but the Free State Constitution had already come into operation on 6 December 1922. This seven-day delay caused the Court in the case of *In re Logue* to conclude that the Free State could give citizenship to everyone on the island (Ó Caoindealbháin, 2006).[18] This rule was not given a legislative basis until the Irish Citizenship and Nationality Act 1935. Later, this wider island-based citizenship was reinforced under both the original text of Article 2 of the 1937 Constitution and its 1998 replacement. Until the British National Act 1948 and the Ireland Act 1949, Irish citizens could also claim UK citizenship.

Nonetheless, to exercise the right to vote would mean that 'the people of Northern Ireland' would have to prove their Irish citizenship (see Chapter Four). The Irish Nationality and Citizenship Act 1956 (amended in 2004) implements Articles 2 and 9 of the Constitution. Article 2 of the Constitution states:

[I]t is the entitlement and birthright of every person born in the island of Ireland, which includes its islands and seas, to be part of the Irish nation. That is also the entitlement of all persons otherwise qualified in accordance with law to be citizens of Ireland.

This creates two categories: those who are part of the Irish nation and those who are citizens, with the latter the only ones bearing citizenship rights. Historically, the Constitution left questions of citizenship to regular law; however, the insertion of Article 9.2

---

[18]   *In re Logue* [1933] 67 ILTR 253.

ended what had previously been a generous citizenship regime. It now does not give citizenship to a person born on the island who does not have at least one parent who is, or is entitled to be, an Irish citizen. This is a change from the previous rules, which entitled all who were born on the island to citizenship regardless of parentage, and will have implications for some people in Northern Ireland after Brexit.

Other than processes of naturalisation and applying for a passport, there are few paths to manifest citizenship. Many amongst the diaspora have taken the opportunity to obtain Irish citizenship post-Brexit because asserting Irish citizenship enables the exercise of EU citizenship rights. This ambiguity which surrounds claims of Irish citizenship is addressed in the Irish Nationality and Citizenship Act 2001 (section 3). It sets out the parameters for citizenship, including for those born in Northern Ireland. Similar parameters were tested in the Irish Supreme Court case of *McGimpsey v Ireland*, where the Court stated that two brothers, both of whom were Unionist politicians from Northern Ireland, were citizens of Ireland even though only one had an Irish passport and neither had made any claim to citizenship.[19] Arguably, this scenario is not changed by the updated law (Nationality and Citizenship Act 2001 (as amended), section 6). That Act states:

> [A] person who is entitled ... to be an Irish citizen shall be an Irish citizen from the date of his or her birth if –
>
> (i) he or she does any act that only an Irish citizen is entitled to do

It goes on to require individuals to have a parent who was an Irish citizen or was entitled to be so, or who was a UK citizen, or who was entitled to reside in Ireland or in Northern Ireland. This ensures that those born in Northern Ireland

---

[19] *McGimpsey v Ireland* [1990] IR 110.

or Ireland to individuals with UK passports are still entitled to Irish citizenship. However, the difficulty that *McGimpsey* highlighted remains. The law requires an individual to do an act that only an Irish citizen is entitled to do, but to do such an act, surely one has to be proven to be an Irish citizen? This all means that in extending the voting franchise to Irish citizens in Northern Ireland, and potentially Great Britain, Ireland would have to devise a method by which to identify citizens. This, of course, could be via a passport; however, obtaining a passport is expensive and it may work more smoothly to administer a different system. Doing so would go some way to ameliorating the democratic deficit created by the extension of EU citizenship rights and their operation in Northern Ireland without representation in the EU Parliament.

Ireland's ongoing EU membership

Ireland's membership of the EEC followed a referendum in 1972 with an overwhelming vote in support (83.1%).[20] Article 29.4.3° of the Irish Constitution provided for EEC law to become part of Irish law and to have primacy over the Constitution (compare this to the UK Constitution's understanding of Parliamentary sovereignty). The evolution of the EEC into the EU and its expanding realm of operation led to a shift in Irish practice regarding new EU treaties. In *Crotty v An Taoiseach*,[21] the Supreme Court decided that the Single European Act significantly developed the authority of the EEC beyond that envisaged by Article 29.4.3°. Since then, all new EU treaties have been put to referendum in Ireland. This continuous (re) insertion of the EU into the Irish Constitution means that Ireland's democratically expressed commitment to the EU is regularly reaffirmed. The nature of the engagement of the Irish

---

[20]   *Third Amendment of the Constitution Act 1972 (Ireland).*

[21]   *Crotty v An Taoiseach* [1987] 1 IR 713.

electorate with EU law has sometimes been questionable, as the double referendums on the Nice Treaty (in 2001 and 2002) and the Lisbon Treaty (in 2008 and 2009) showed (Cahill, 2008). Ireland's regular constitutional interaction with its membership nonetheless contrasts with the UK, where the pressure created by limited engagement built towards Brexit.

Ireland is both domestically and internationally required to fully implement EU law and it takes priority over Irish law, including the GFA-based provisions in Articles 2, 3 and 29.7. EU case law has also placed EU law obligations above any other international obligations, including those to the United Nations (UN) and the Council of Europe.[22] Both EU law and the GFA come under Article 29 of the Irish Constitution. Under the Irish Constitution, EU law would therefore legally take precedence over the GFA.

Although this scenario is hypothetical while all parties to Brexit accept the significance of the GFA, it is important to consider a situation where Ireland may have to choose between complying with the GFA and its EU obligations. At the domestic level, EU law would take legal precedence. At the international level, Ireland would have to choose. In the case of a dispute, the case could not come before the International Court of Justice (ICJ) due to exclusions that Ireland has submitted regarding Northern Ireland. Should Ireland choose the GFA, it is likely that the CJEU would find Ireland in breach of its EU obligations. A helpful option to see off this potentially awkward situation would be for Ireland to negotiate a protocol on the GFA with the EU. It has done so previously regarding abortion and neutrality, and the UK and Ireland have agreed a similar protocol regarding the Common Travel Area.[23]

---

[22] C-584/10 P, C-593/10 P and C-595/10 P, *European Commission v Yassin Abdullah Kadi* (19 March 2013).

[23] *Protocol on the Concerns of the Irish People on the Treaty of Lisbon* 2.3.2013 Official Journal of the European Union L 60/131.

The time required to negotiate such an agreement potentially makes the exercise politically urgent. Nonetheless, the draft Withdrawal Agreement incorporates the GFA into its Protocol on Ireland/Northern Ireland. Although the Protocol is still subject to negotiation, the GFA is explicitly affirmed by both the UK and EU as needing 'to be protected in all parts'. For that to hold true, the settlement arrived at between the UK and the EU must comply with the EU treaties and the principles stemming from them. If there is a clash between the core EU treaties and any future UK–EU treaty that 'protects' the GFA, the CJEU's existing case law suggests that EU law would 'win' that clash (if it cannot be interpreted away). The likely outcome of such a clash would be the CJEU requiring the EU to renegotiate its agreement with the UK, if not to disapply it outright.

Modifying the GFA under international law

One eventuality, which we have yet to cover, is amending the GFA to reflect Brexit priorities. Successor treaties, treaty amendments and fundamental changes in circumstances all provide avenues for altering a treaty. International law allows treaties to be suspended or ended by another treaty, and this is an option that is available to both governments (*Vienna Convention on the Law of Treaties 1969*, Article 59). The same principles of international law also allow for subsequent treaties to change the provisions of an earlier treaty (*Vienna Convention on the Law of Treaties 1969*, Article 59). This is a route that the Irish and UK governments have used since the Anglo-Irish Treaty 1921.[24]

If a new bilateral treaty was agreed between London and Dublin, the GFA could be terminated (just as the Anglo-Irish Agreement of 1985 was terminated by the GFA). However, it is all-but-inconceivable that such an alteration would occur

---

[24] *Government of Ireland Act 1920 (UK)*; Treaty between Great Britain and Ireland, 1921.

without the consent of Northern Ireland's political parties. While standard international law allows for changes to treaties, the GFA is not a standard agreement. The major part of the GFA treaty was agreed between Northern Ireland's political parties, meaning that not only is the political viability of amendments doubtful, but such changes would also strike against the special nature of the GFA as a peace agreement.

The citizenship referendum in Ireland is a useful case study of how constitutional changes can be incorporated while respecting the GFA. The referendum approved the Nineteenth Amendment, partly reversing changes that had been made to Ireland's Constitution in response to the GFA. To maintain its international obligations, the Irish government first asked for the UK government's agreement to the changes through an Interpretative Declaration to the effect '[T]hat this proposed change to the Constitution is not a breach of the ... Agreement or the continuing obligation of good faith in the implementation of the said Agreement'.[25] Through this declaration, the Irish government reaffirmed its responsibility for safeguarding the GFA's institutions and principles (Flanagan, 2015). The UK government could seek a similar declaration at this important point for the GFA to demonstrate that it remains legally committed to the Agreement and intends to continue in good faith.

What all of this means is that the UK government cannot act unilaterally. Any changes must be done through renegotiation with the Irish government and, given the circumstances, with the parties in Northern Ireland. It would be very difficult to reopen parts of the 1998 settlement in isolation. If the UK acted unilaterally, several options would be available under international law (*Vienna Convention on the Law of Treaties*

---

[25] Citizenship Referendum: Interpretative Declaration by the Irish and British Governments regarding the British Irish Agreement, *Dáil Debate*, Vol. 583 No. 6 (21 April 2004).

1969, Article 60). If the Irish government considered the UK's unilateral act to be a 'material breach' of its obligations, Ireland would be entitled to respond. An 'internationally wrongful act' can be an act or omission that can be traced to a state and that is a breach of its international obligations (International Law Commission, 2001). The internal political conditions or domestic law of a country are irrelevant to whether or not there has been a breach. Any claims that may be made about the need for UK institutions to breach the GFA to address the demands of the electorate in the Brexit referendum are irrelevant to this area of international law.

Although the GFA includes no rules for settling disputes between the UK and Ireland, some other options remain open to Ireland in these circumstances. One option would be to terminate or suspend the whole or part of the treaty. It is difficult, however, to see how this response would aid the Irish government's efforts to apply pressure upon the UK to maintain its GFA obligations. Another option – the ICJ – would likely not, however, provide an avenue for redress. Both states, in making declarations of compulsory jurisdiction (recognising the ICJ's authority), included qualifications that likely exclude the other. Ireland allows for all disputes to be heard at the ICJ, except those that arise between it and the UK regarding Northern Ireland. The UK's declaration excludes 'any dispute with the government of any other country which is or has been a Member of the Commonwealth'.[26] Although it is debatable whether Ireland was ever part of the modern Commonwealth, together, these declarations prevent the ICJ option. The most likely option, however, lies with the Withdrawal Agreement itself. As we have already seen, the draft Withdrawal Agreement's Protocol on Ireland/Northern Ireland builds the GFA into its terms. If the UK government or Parliament did act in a way

---

[26] International Court of Justice (2018). Both states' declarations are available at: http://www.icj-cij.org/en/declarations.

that threatened the GFA's terms, it would be a breach of the GFA and the Withdrawal Agreement and could lead to the issue being tackled by whatever dispute resolution process results from the Brexit negotiations.

Conclusion

For large parts of the past century, the drivers for constitutional change in the Northern Ireland context have often been bleak. Against the backdrop of partition and sectarian conflict, Brexit might seem to rank as a relatively benign force for change. However, it is one that has unsettled an already-fragile governance order. To borrow a line from Tony Blair (2001): 'the kaleidoscope has been shaken, the pieces are in flux'. By itself, this is nothing new. The interactions between Ireland's and the UK's constitutional orders over the centuries have frequently been characterised by dynamism (Carty, 1996, p 158). It nonetheless emphasises the need to keep some anchors in these arrangements, which explains why Brexit negotiations keep coming back to the GFA as a benchmark. Moreover, while Ireland, like other countries, will need to adapt to Brexit, the strains upon the UK Constitution will be much greater. Constitutional adaptation must take place at a time when the policymaking organs of the UK's governance order are already stretched by the enormity of the task of making Brexit a reality. It is little wonder that since the Joint Report was concluded, talk has turned to the UK stretching the length of transitional periods in which EU law will continue to apply in full and constitutional change can, at least, be paced.

SEVEN

A place apart

[T]he exact same benefits. It's bollocks. It always has been bollocks and it remains it ... (Barry Gardiner, MP, quoted in BBC, 2018b)

The special status of post-Brexit Northern Ireland

The Phase 1 Joint Report sets up a special status for post-Brexit Northern Ireland, providing for distinct regulatory arrangements, citizenship rules and rights protections (which, in some instances, could be extended to cover the whole of the UK). These special arrangements are bolted onto a peace process that Tony Blair (2006) famously characterised as having no agreed end point. Nationalists and Unionists support irreconcilable constitutional futures for Northern Ireland; there must be either the reunification of Ireland or a continued place for Northern Ireland within the UK. All of which leads to one big question, colouring our entire discussion of Brexit: will the Brexit settlement advantage one of these end points?

The tail wagging the dog?

The adaptability of the European Union

The EU is a club made up of states, or it has been up to now. For some, the question is whether the EU can develop beyond this point: 'the EU must be regarded as an organization of men and women as opposed to a simple union of states, and one that accommodates different kinds of representative institutions' (Della Cananea, 2010, p 300). The flexibility demonstrated towards key concepts in EU law in its proposed Brexit solutions for Northern Ireland suggests that it is, indeed, embracing this challenge. Northern Ireland has amply demonstrated its capacity to reshape two national constitutions, and in Brexit, it is forcing a supranational body to confront what kind of organisation it aspires to be and what being one of its citizens means.

It is a favourite theme of Brexiteers that the EU is giving up nothing during the current negotiations. However, just how far the EU has come with regard to Northern Ireland is clear in the Commission's initial mission statement on the Brexit negotiations:

> [T]he Union is committed to continuing to support peace, stability and reconciliation on the island of Ireland. Nothing in the Agreement should undermine the objectives and commitments set out in the Good Friday Agreement in all its parts and its related implementing agreements; the unique circumstances and challenges on the island of Ireland will require flexible and imaginative solutions. *Negotiations should in particular aim to avoid the creation of a hard border on the island of Ireland, while respecting the integrity of the Union legal order.* (European Commission, 2018b, para 14, emphasis added)

The Phase 1 Agreement affirmed that Northern Ireland would enjoy special status after Brexit and started to flesh out the nature of what that meant for the EU but also for the UK and Ireland: no diminution of human rights standards; regulatory alignment between Northern Ireland and Ireland, the facilitation of trade in goods and services on the island of Ireland; and EU citizenship and fundamental rights for the people of Northern Ireland. This solution stands to redefine core tenets of the EU legal order.

The most important provisions of the Phase 1 Report stated that even if no final deal is reached, the sections on Northern Ireland would be binding. In short, the post-Brexit geopolitical landscape of Northern Ireland has been outlined, and now the task is filling in this picture in more detail. Dublin, London and Brussels each play a role in setting out the detail of what post-Brexit Northern Ireland will look like, but Northern Ireland (even without a functioning Assembly) provides its own force in these negotiations, and is no stranger to being a distinct constitutional space.

Northern Ireland: a constitutional conundrum

The UK Constitution is, in some respects, a defensive arrangement. In *Law and Public Opinion*, Dicey confided to his readership that he saw no place in the world for small states, which would inevitably be swallowed up by larger ones in the imperial world of 19th-/early 20th-century international relations. A unitary constitution with power centralised in Westminster was the only way to stave off national annihilation (Dicey, 1917, p 323). As with other things he wrote, he turned out (in the long run) to be wrong. Ireland was able to break away from the UK and establish its own statehood, a status that is strengthened by its ability to act as part of the EU.

Northern Ireland could be described as a law unto itself, requiring special constitutional settlements, from Home Rule to the Anglo-Irish Agreement to the Good Friday Agreement (GFA). Although many UK scholars insist that almost all of these developments were sealed off from the rest of the UK

Constitution – 'what happens in Northern Ireland stays in Northern Ireland' (King, 2009, p 185) – this is an essentially London-centric view of the UK Constitution. Partition reshaped the UK as much as it created Ireland, Home Rule in Northern Ireland was a first attempt at devolution, and the Anglo-Irish Agreement and the GFA challenged classic ideas of the state and citizenship. The agreement of special post-Brexit arrangements, however, stands to make Northern Ireland an even more radical constitutional space.

The conclusion of the Phase 1 talks brought Northern Ireland to centre stage, bringing with it suggestions that the tail is somehow wagging the dog. The Conservatives' reliance upon the Democratic Unionist Party's (DUP's) confidence-and-supply agreement at Westminster required that the deal be accepted by Arlene Foster, and her last-minute jitters about how it would be perceived by her supporters generated days of frantic extra negotiations in December 2017. However, Northern Ireland's special place within Brexit is not the product of the DUP's machinations. The Phase 1 deal has the potential to reshape EU law, the UK Constitution and Northern Ireland's status. It also necessitates a change of constitutional narrative; Northern Ireland cannot be treated as peripheral to Brexit.

Intertwining the GFA into Brexit

The GFA: an end, not a beginning

The GFA provided a platform for ending the violence of the Northern Ireland conflict, and it addressed sources of conflict by measures such as extending anti-discrimination protections, human rights protections and police reform. It obliged the divided communities to work together in the Northern Ireland Assembly/Executive, but power sharing always assumed that the two communities were a fixed feature of life in Northern Ireland and, indeed, operated to reinforce that division. It fixed in place a system that ignored those who did not fit well into those two communities or who those two communities rejected.

In the new peace, visible identity differences became an insistent feature of life in Northern Ireland. Wearing a Northern Ireland soccer strip or a GAA jersey after decades of studiously concealing identity provided a moment of glorious release for the people of Northern Ireland, but identity politics also manifested itself in flashpoint parades and language debates that ultimately eroded the capacity for effective power sharing. For others, this era has been marked by the rejection of 'two-community' divisions in Pride and Alliance for Choice marches in Northern Ireland (Fenton, 2018, pp 216–18). The referendums in Ireland introducing marriage equality in 2015 and repealing the 8th Amendment on abortion in 2018 have galvanised a larger section of Northern Ireland's society into demanding comparable rights to those available in Dublin and London.

The GFA does not stop Brexit, and even if it *could*, it is certainly worth asking whether it *should*. However, the GFA was endorsed by popular referendum in two jurisdictions and, as such, has as much legitimacy as the Brexit vote. It envisaged Northern Ireland as being in the EU, even if it was not explicitly defined in terms of EU membership. The GFA therefore conditions how Brexit impacts on Northern Ireland. For instance, it obliges the maintenance of equivalent rights protections between Northern Ireland and the Republic of Ireland. The equivalence requirement does not envisage exact mirroring of rights on either side of the Irish border, as debates over reproductive rights and equal marriage provisions illustrate, but it does work against a free-for-all Brexit that wrenches Northern Ireland out of the all-island framework.

The people of Northern Ireland: canny actors or big wee'uns?

Whereas 'We the People …' in the US Constitution has poetic elegance, there remains an awkwardness in the phase 'the people of Northern Ireland'. The GFA recognised a people defined by their differences; it did not bond Unionists and Nationalists, but hoped that those bonds would emerge in the context of power sharing. The Phase 1 Joint Report holds out EU law rights to this group. Under EU law, many rights are tied to residence in the EU. Rights such as freedom to establish an EU company do not extend to an EU citizen resident in New York, but under the Joint Report, they will extend to an EU citizen resident in Belfast.

In other words, the Phase 1 Report does not, as it says, simply affirm the GFA. It is a new development that could be as significant a constitutional moment for Northern Ireland as the GFA before it; a beginning and not an ending. Even if this is not the intention of negotiators, the Withdrawal Agreement could quietly forge a common identity based on positive benefits for the people of Northern Ireland and potentially smuggle this identity into existence while everyone is fixated on other aspects of Brexit.

DUP politicians Sammy Wilson and Ian Paisley Jr have suggested that the people of Northern Ireland should be canny actors in this new game, collecting passports for all occasions. Their assumption is that this act will not impact on identity; people will take an Irish passport to access their EU law rights, and a UK passport to fully secure their rights in the remainder of the UK if the Common Travel Area (CTA) becomes problematic after Brexit, but doing so will have no impact on their being British or Irish. However, now that being 'of Northern Ireland' is of itself something valuable, the likelihood is that if Belfast emerges as a hub in which companies seek to take advantage of being in the best of both worlds in UK/EU terms, these traditional ideas of identity will shift, at least for individuals who perceive benefits to this new reality.

To gain this new identity, what do the people of Northern Ireland have to give up? Northern Ireland will exist as a polity upon which EU rules are imposed, but without having a direct say in their creation unless Ireland extends its franchise for European elections. The DUP's current leverage within the UK Parliament is fleeting, and will likely not outlast another general election. Furthermore, the space for devolved government seems as uncertain as it ever has since 1998. Northern Ireland will sit at the confluence of multiple constitutional orders, but its people will potentially be left as 'big wee'uns', with little ability to influence many of the laws that govern them. Constituent power might be neutered, and the decision-making space bureaucratised, but if this settlement works, it will not necessarily shift Northern Ireland towards Dublin or London; it could maintain it as a place apart.

'It's the economy (stupid)'

Brexit will reshape identities, both constitutional and personal, but the UK and the EU seem to be committed to preserving rights and ensuring that there are no new borders on the island of Ireland. Readers could therefore be forgiven for thinking that if a Withdrawal Agreement is struck, nothing will *actually* change for businesses in Northern Ireland, but the reality is much more complicated.

Let's say that we arrive at a successful Withdrawal Agreement. The UK government has, to date, maintained that it wants any 'special status' for Northern Ireland to be, at most, temporary, and that it will ultimately endeavour to get rid of the 'hard border' by some other means, like 'Max Fac'. Up until the White Paper of July 2018 ministers also touted the ability to set its own product and agricultural regulations as one of the main advantages of Brexit. A particularly memorable example was Boris Johnson enthusing that Brexit will mean 'doing wonderful things with our own regulations to promote organic carrots', misunderstanding a reporter's question about clarity rather than carrots (Bartlett, 2018). The EU has, of course, responded by making any deal contingent on the UK not seeking to undercut the EU by introducing the world's 'least red tape' regulatory regime (European Council, 2018).

Somewhere between these two 'trade' positions, we will find the future – and the future will have an impact on business in Northern Ireland in practice, even if there is no hard customs border. For Brexit to make *any* sense, the UK will need to make itself competitive – and if it cannot do so by scrapping all 'red tape' on products, it will do so through whatever international deals it can sign with other countries. This may make it more attractive for some of Northern Ireland's businesses to look away from Ireland and the EU, but less so for the agri-food industry that makes up so much of the Northern Ireland economy as it relies on freshness and short transport distances to make its products valuable (Allen, 2016).

Something will have to be done to make Northern Ireland's milk and chickens saleable, even though farming activity (and, consequently, the price of products) will no longer enjoy the considerable support of the EU's Common Agricultural Policy. The UK government's pledge to keep that kind of subsidy in place until 2022 is all well and good, but it does not provide for a sustainable future for Northern Ireland's agri-food industry – and despite aspects of agricultural policy being devolved to Northern Ireland, any funding for subsidies will have to keep coming from Westminster if they are not coming from the EU (BBC, 2018c).

We risk ending up with an open land border that sees a lot of business from the EU to the UK, but not an awful lot in another direction. The conclusion of a successful 'trade deal' that keeps that border open might end one Northern Ireland-centred Brexit panic, but it cannot possibly counteract all the economic upheaval that Brexit will cause (Connelly, 2018a, pp 41–3).

Finding love in a hopeless place

The EU was long seen by Northern Ireland Nationalists as a means of diluting UK sovereignty over Northern Ireland. The DUP's visceral rejection of the EU (best summarised by Ian Paisley Sr's exhortation to milk the Brussels cow dry before slitting its throat) is, by contrast, conditioned by their regard for anything that reaffirms UK sovereignty as good for Unionism. The Brexit negotiations, however, indicate that new barriers could emerge between Great Britain and Northern Ireland, throwing those certainties into doubt. Talk of national sovereignty ignores both the political reality of Europe and how Northern Ireland has, over the last century, become increasingly distinct from Ireland and the remainder of the UK.

The prioritisation of an open border between Northern Ireland and the Republic of Ireland by both Dublin and London suggests that the status quo largely suits both. Indeed, while Dublin secured a guarantee that future unification of Ireland within the EU would be treated like the reunification of Germany, it has also maintained that this would only occur under the terms of the GFA (as confirmed by the Irish Constitution). The Phase 1 Agreement does not affect the GFA's consent principle, nor does it change the consent requirements of Ireland's Constitution. Any shift in such a direction is likely to be gradual. The 56% support in Northern Ireland for remaining within the EU, even accompanied by the growth of the non-Unionist vote share in the 2017 Assembly elections, do not presage an imminent end to partition.

Effective peace agreements rely on all sides being able to sell the deal as a victory to their supporters, whereas ineffective ones sustain a narrative of winners and losers. The GFA arrangements have proven to be amazingly resilient despite the DUP's strident efforts to present them as a defeat for Unionism. It has helped that the DUP has been obliged to buy into the process since the St Andrews 'renegotiation'. As a result, the

GFA provides a workable foundation on which the current negotiations can build. Can this provide a sustainable framework for governance after Brexit? Perhaps, but the lesson from 1998 is that some actors will undoubtedly seek political advantage by destabilising such arrangements. The danger is that the UK Government continues to try to have its cake and eat it too. The July 2018 White Paper prioritises both the Union (in terms of the constitutional integrity of the UK) and the need for special arrangements for Northern Ireland after Brexit. It envisages the UK and EU adopting a 'responsible approach to avoiding a hard border between Northern Ireland and Ireland, in a way that respects the constitutional and economic integrity of the UK and the autonomy of the EU' (May, 2018d, p 7). These aspirations will, however, prove hard to fit together, given that the EU and UK negotiating positions on the extent of "special status" for Northern Ireland post-Brexit remain far removed from each other.

After Brexit, Northern Ireland could become a place apart, where EU citizens benefit from EU membership even outside the Union, and where a combination of the ability of its people to maintain multiple citizenships and regulatory alignment with EU rules allow its politicians to restructure its economy. To get there, however, compromise will be needed. Northern Ireland remains sandwiched uncomfortably between two unions. Brexit must therefore address the reality of the GFA as a peace settlement, the reality of people's lives near a land border and even the reality that Northern Ireland is a place where imaginative solutions can – and do – happen.

Bibliography

A v Secretary of State for the Home Department [2004] UKHL 56

Act of Union 1800 (40 Geo.3, c.38). London: HMSO.

Agreement at St Andrews (2006) [Online]. [Accessed 25 May 2018]. Available from: https://assets.publishing.service.gov.uk/government/uploads/system/uploads/attachment_data/file/136651/st_andrews_agreement-2.pdf

Agreement between Great Britain and the Irish Free State, amending and supplementing the Treaty of December 6, 1921, between Great Britain and the Irish Free State, Signed at London, December 3, 1925. *League of Nations Treaty Series*, 44 (1088).

Agreement between the Government of the United Kingdom of Great Britain and Northern Ireland and the Government of Ireland (with annexes) (Belfast/Good Friday Agreement) (1998) 2114 UNTS 473.

Allegretti, A. (2018) Labour MP Barry Gardiner apologises for suggesting 'shibboleth' Good Friday Agreement is 'played up'. *Sky News*. [Online]. 10 April. [Accessed 25 May 2018]. Available from: https://news.sky.com/story/labour-mp-barry-gardiner-apologises-for-suggesting-shibboleth-good-friday-agreement-is-played-up-11324938

Allen, M. (2016) Northern Ireland's agri-food sector – background and possible 'Brexit' considerations. [Online]. Northern Ireland Assembly Research. [Accessed 25 May 2018]. Available from: http://www.niassembly.gov.uk/globalassets/documents/raise/publications/2016-2021/2016/aera/6616.pdf

Amnesty International. (2017) A matter of routine: the use of immigration detention in the UK. [Online]. [Accessed 10 January 2018]. Available from: https://www.amnesty.org.uk/resources/matter-routine-use-immigration-detention-uk-0

Anglo-Irish Agreement 1985. London: HMSO.

Armstrong, K. (2017) *Brexit Time: Leaving The EU – Why, How and When?,* Cambridge: Cambridge University Press.

Arthur, P. (2000) *Special Relationships: Britain, Ireland and the Northern Ireland Problem,* Belfast: Blackstaff Press.

Articles of Agreement for a Treaty between Great Britain and Ireland 1921. [Online]. [Accessed 28 June 2018]. Available from: http://www.difp.ie/docs/1921/Anglo-Irish-Treaty/214.htm

Attorney General v X [1992] 1 IR 1.

Barnier, M. (2017) Speech at the Joint Houses of the Oireachtas. [Online]. 11 May, Joint Houses of the Oireachtas, Dublin. [Accessed 28 May 2018]. Available from: http://europa.eu/rapid/press-release_SPEECH-17-1276_en.htm

Barnier, M. (2018) Press Statement by Michel Barnier following the publication of the Draft Withdrawal Agreement between the EU and the UK. [Online]. 28 February, Brussels. [Accessed 25 May 2018]. Available from: http://europa.eu/rapid/press-release_STATEMENT-18-1402_en.htm

Barrington, D. (1957) Uniting Ireland. *Studies: An Irish Quarterly Review* 46: 379.

Bartels, L. (2013) Human rights and sustainable development obligations in EU free trade agreements. *Legal Issues of Economic Integration* 40: 297.

Bartlett, N. (2018) Sex tourism, organic carrots and Toblerone cabinets – 9 surprising moments from Boris Johnson's Brexit speech. *Mirror.* [Online]. 14 February. [Accessed 25 May 2018]. Available from: https://www.mirror.co.uk/news/politics/sex-tourism-organic-carrots-toblerone-12024864

Bate, A. and Bellis, A. (2017) Right to rent: private landlords' duty to carry out immigration status checks. House of Commons Library, SN07025.

BBC (British Broadcasting Corporation). (2016) Immigration: May rejects points-based system for EU nationals. BBC News. [Online]. 5 September. [Accessed 10 January 2018]. Available from: http://www.bbc.co.uk/news/uk-politics-37271420

BBC. (2018a) UK–EU customs partnership 'still on table'. [Online]. [Accessed 25 May 2018]. Available from: http://www.bbc.co.uk/news/uk-politics-44021119

BBC. (2018b) Labour's Barry Gardiner rubbished key Brexit policy. [Online]. [Accessed 25 May 2018]. Available from: http://www.bbc.co.uk/news/uk-politics-43710728

BBC. (2018c) Post-Brexit farming funding set out by Michael Gove. [Online]. [Accessed 25 May 2018]. Available from: http://www.bbc.co.uk/news/uk-politics-42559845

Beckett, J.C. (1971) Northern Ireland. *Journal of Contemporary History* 6: 121.

Belassa, B. (2013) *The Theory of Economic Integration* (5th edn). Abingdon: Routledge.

Bell, C. and Cavanaugh, K. (1998) Constructive ambiguity or internal self-determination – self-determination, group accommodation, and the Belfast Agreement. Fordham International Law Journal 22: 1345.

Blair, T. (2001) Labour Party Conference speech. *The Guardian*. [Online]. 2 October. [Accessed 28 May 2018]. Available from: https://www.theguardian.com/politics/2001/oct/02/labourconference.labour7

Blair, T. (2006) PM's foreign policy speech. [Online]. 26 May, Georgetown. [Accessed 25 May 2018]. Available from: http://webarchive.nationalarchives.gov.uk/20060530093341/http://www.pm.gov.uk/output/Page9549.asp

Bloomer, N. and Jeraj, S. (2017) Met Police hands victims of crime over to the Home Office for immigration enforcement. [Online]. [Accessed 10 January 2018]. Available from: http://www.politics.co.uk/news/2017/04/05/met-police-hands-victims-of-crime-over-to-the-home-office

Boffey, D. (2017) Irish report shows lack of respect in EU for UK's handling of Brexit. *The Guardian*. [Online]. 23 November. [Accessed 28 May 2018]. Available from: https://www.theguardian.com/politics/2017/nov/23/irish-report-shows-eu-lack-of-respect-for-uk-handling-of-brexit

Boland v An Taoiseach [1974] IR 338.

Brennan, C., Purdy, R. and Hjerp, P. (2017) Political, economic and environmental crisis in Northern Ireland: the true cost of environmental governance failures and opportunities for reform. *Northern Ireland Legal Quarterly* 68: 123.

Bridges, G. *Hansard* HL Deb. vol.773 col.376, 24 May 2016.

British Nationality Act 1948 (UK) (11&12 Geo.6, c.56). London: HMSO.

Brokenshire, J. (2017) Secretary of State's speech to the European Policy Centre. [Online]. 10 April. [Accessed 25 May 2018]. Available from: https://www.gov.uk/government/speeches/secretary-of-states-speech-to-the-european-policy-centre

C-26/62 *Van Gend en Loos v Nederlandse Administratie der Belastingen* [1963] ECR 1.

C-120/78 *Rewe-Zentral AG v Bundesmonopolverwaltung für Branntwein* EU:C:1979:42.

C-168/91 *Konstantinidis v Stadt Altensteig-Standesamt* [1993] ECR 1-1198.

C-203/15 and C-698/15 *Secretary of State for the Home Department v Watson* [2017] 2 CMLR 30 (Grand Chamber, CJEU).

C-397-403/01 *Pfeiffer v Deutsches Rotes Kreuz* EU:C:2004:584.

C-399/11 *Melloni v Ministerio Fiscal* [2013] 2 CMLR 43 (Grand Chamber, CJEU).

C-584/10 P, C-593/10 P and C-595/10 P, *European Commission v Yassin Abdullah Kadi* (19 March 2013).

Cabinet Office. (2018) Technical Note: Temporary Customs Arrangements. [Online.] [Accessed 28 June 2018]. Available from: https://assets.publishing.service.gov.uk/government/uploads/system/uploads/attachment_data/file/714656/Technical_note_temporary_customs_arrangement.pdf

Cahill M. (2008) Ireland's constitutional amendability and Europe's constitutional ambition: the Lisbon referendum in context. *German Law Journal* 9: 1191.

Calvert, H. (1968) *Constitutional Law in Northern Ireland: A Study in Regional Government.* London: Stevens & Sons.

Campbell, J. (2017) Brexit: what is regulatory alignment? *BBC News.* [Online]. 5 December. [Accessed 25 May 2018]. Available from: http://www.bbc.co.uk/news/uk-northern-ireland-42240339

Campbell, L. (2017) *Beyond Brexit – Beyond Borders Mutual Assistance in Policing and Investigating Organised Crime.* [Online]. Durham: Durham University Centre for Criminal Law and Criminal Justice. [Accessed 1 June 2018]. Available from: https://www.dur.ac.uk/resources/law/research/BrexitExecutiveSummary.pdf

Carty, A. (1996) *Was Ireland Conquered? International Law and the Irish Question.* London: Pluto Press.

Charter of Fundamental Rights of the European Union, 18 December 2000. [Online]. 2000/C 364/01. [Accessed 1 June 2018]. Available from: http://www.europarl.europa.eu/charter/pdf/text_en.pdf

Chubb, B. (1986) Britain and Irish constitutional development. In: Drudy P.J. ed. *Ireland and Britain since 1922.* Cambridge: Cambridge University Press, p. 21.

Citizenship Referendum: Interpretative Declaration by the Irish and British Governments regarding the British Irish Agreement, *Dáil Debate*, vol.583, no.6, 21 April 2004.

Clarke, V. (2018) Trimble says Irish Brexit challenges could be solved 'in half an hour'. *The Irish Times.* [Online]. 10 April. [Accessed 28 May 2018]. Available from: https://www.irishtimes.com/news/politics/trimble-says-irish-brexit-challenges-could-be-solved-in-half-an-hour-1.3456791

Cloatre, E. and Enright, M. (2017) On the perimeter of the lawful: enduring illegality in the Irish Family Planning Movement, 1972–1985. *Journal of Law and Society* 44(4).

Colson, T. (2018) Here's what the new Brexit application process for EU citizens will look like. *Business Insider UK*. [Online]. 1 May. [Accessed 10 January 2018]. Available from: http://uk.businessinsider.com/everything-you-need-to-know-about-the-new-brexit-application-smartphone-process-for-eu-citizens-2018-4

Connelly, T. (2018a) *Brexit and Ireland: The Dangers, the Opportunities, and the Inside Story of the Irish Response*. Dublin: Penguin Ireland.

Connelly, T. (2018b) The Irish Protocol: how Theresa May's backstop somersault is fraught with danger. *RTÉ News*. [Online]. 19 May. [Accessed 25 May 2018]. Available from: https://www.rte.ie/news/brexit/2018/0518/964505-tony-connelly-brexit/

Conservative Party, *Forward Together: The Conservative Manifesto* (2017).

Constitutional Review Group (1996) Dublin: Stationery Office.

Constitution of Ireland – Bunreacht na hÉireann 1937.

Constitution of the Irish Free State (Saorstát Eireann) 1922.Corporation Tax (Northern Ireland) Act 2015. (c.21). London: HMSO.

Cox, G. *Hansard* HC Deb. vol.632, col.1104, 6 December 2017.

Craig, P. and De Burca, G. (2015) *EU Law: Text, Cases and Materials*. Oxford: Oxford University Press.

Crangle, J. (2018) 'Left to fend for themselves': immigration, race relations and the state in twentieth century Northern Ireland. *Historical Studies in Ethnicity, Migration and Diaspora* 36.

Crotty v An Taoiseach [1987] 1 IR 713.

Daly, E. (2012) *Religion, Law and the Irish State: The Constitutional Framework in Context*. Dublin: Clarus Press.

Davis, D. (2017a) Interview: *Peston on Sunday*. [Online]. 14 May, London. [Accessed 28 May 2018]. Available from: https://www.youtube.com/watch?t=3s&v=RotUXuOlaac&app=desktop

Davis, D. (2017b) *Hansard* HC Deb. vol.630, col.963, 2 November 2017.

Davis, D. (2018) Statement: EU–UK Article 50 negotiations. [Online]. 19 March, Brussels. [Accessed 28 May 2018]. Available from: https://www.gov.uk/government/news/david-davis-statement-eu-uk-article-50-negotiations-brussels-monday-19-march-2018

De Clercq, W. (1987) Speech by Mr De Clercq at the EEC/EFTA Ministerial Meeting – Interlaken. [Online]. 20 May, Interlaken. [Accessed 28 May 2018]. Available from: http://europa.eu/rapid/press-release_SPEECH-87-32_en.htm

De Hert, P. and Papakonstantinou, V. (2017) The rich UK contribution to the field of EU data protection: let's not go for 'third country' status after Brexit. *Computer Law & Security Review* 33: 354.

Della Cananea, G. (2010) Is European constitutionalism really 'multilevel'? *Heidelberg Journal of International Law* 70.

Della Sala, V. (2010) Political myth, mythology and the European Union. *Journal of Common Market Studies* 48: 1.

Denton, G. and Fahey, T. (1993) *The Northern Ireland Land Boundary 1923–1992*. Belfast: The Universities Press.

Department for Work and Pensions. (2014) Minimum earnings threshold for EEA migrants introduced. [Online]. [Accessed 26 May 2018]. Available from: https://www.gov.uk/government/news/minimum-earnings-threshold-for-eea-migrants-introduced

Department of Housing, Planning, Community and Local Government (2016) Referendum results 1937–2015. [Online]. [Accessed 28 May 2018]. Available from: http://www.housing.gov.ie/sites/default/files/migrated-files/en/Publications/LocalGovernment/Voting/referendum_results_1937-2015.pdf

DExEU (Department for Exiting the European Union). (2017) Charter of Fundamental Rights of the EU: right by right analysis. [Online]. [Accessed 1 June 2018]. Available from: https://assets.publishing.service.gov.uk/government/uploads/system/uploads/attachment_data/file/664891/05122017_Charter_Analysis_FINAL_VERSION.pdf

DExEU. (2018) EU citizens arriving in the UK during the implementation period. [Online]. [Accessed 25 May 2018]. Available from: https://www.gov.uk/government/publications/eu-citizens-arriving-in-the-uk-during-the-implementation-period/eu-citizens-arriving-in-the-uk-during-the-implementation-period

Dicey, A.V. (1885) *Introduction to the Study of the Law of the Constitution*. Basingstoke: Macmillan.

Dicey, A.V. (1917) *Lectures on the Relation Between Law & Public Opinion in England: During the Nineteenth Century*. Basingstoke: Macmillan.

Dixon, P. (1994) *Northern Ireland: The Politics of War and Peace* (1st edn). London: Palgrave Macmillan.

Dodds, N. *Hansard* HC Deb. vol.606, col.34, 22 February 2016.

Donnelly, M. (2018) Speech to King's College London. *OpenDemocracyUK*. [Online]. 9 March. [Accessed 1 June 2018]. Available from: https://www.opendemocracy.net/uk/martin-donnelly/liam-fox-s-brexit-aims-require-not-so-much-skilled-negotiating-team-as-fairy-godm

Dorr, N. (2017) *The Search for Peace in Northern Ireland: Sunningdale*. Dublin: Royal Irish Academy.

Doyle, J. (2018) Boris goes to war with May over her 'crazy' Brexit trade plan: Foreign Secretary warns the customs partnership would leave Britain tied to EU with 'new web of bureaucracy'. *Daily Mail*. [Online]. 8 May. [Accessed 25 May 2018]. Available from: http://www.dailymail.co.uk/news/article-5701033/Boris-Johnson-savages-Downing-Streets-post-Brexit-trade-plans.html

Draft Agreement Text (passed from DUP to Sinn Féin). (2018) [Online]. [Accessed 25 May 2018]. Available from: http://eamonnmallie.com/2018/02/full-draft-agreement-text/

EEC Commission Regulation No 1062/87 of 27 March 1987 on provisions for the implementation of the Community transit procedure and for certain simplifications of that procedure.

Equality Act 2010 (UK). (c.15). London: HMSO.

EU Council Decision of the European Council 2002/772/EC of 25 June 2002 and 23 September 2002. [Online]. [Accessed 28 June 218]. Available from: https://eur-lex.europa.eu/legal-content/en/ALL/?uri=CELEX%3A32002D0772

EU Council Decision 2006/697/EC of 27 June 2006 on the signing of the Agreement between the European Union and the Republic of Iceland and the Kingdom of Norway on the surrender procedure between the Member States of the European Union and Iceland and Norway. [Online]. [Accessed 28 June 2018]. Available from: https://eur-lex.europa.eu/legal-content/EN/ALL/?uri=celex%3A32006D0697

EU Council Decision 2014/835/EU of 27 November 2014 on the conclusion of the Agreement between the European Union and the Republic of Iceland and the Kingdom of Norway on the surrender procedure between the Member States of the European Union and Iceland and Norway. [Online]. [Accessed 1 June 2018]. Available from: https://eur-lex.europa.eu/legal-content/EN/TXT/?uri=CELEX%3A32014D0835

EU Council Directive 1993/109/EC of 6 December 1993 laying down detailed arrangements for the exercise of the right to vote and stand as a candidate in elections to the European Parliament. [Online]. [Accessed 28 June 2018]. Available from: https://eur-lex.europa.eu/legal-content/en/ALL/?uri=celex:31993L0109

EU Council Directive 2000/78/EC of 27 November 2000 establishing a general framework for equal treatment in employment and occupation. [Online]. [Accessed 31 May 2018]. Available from: https://eur-lex.europa.eu/LexUriServ/LexUriServ.do?uri=CELEX:32000L0078:en:HTML

EU Council Directive 2004/38/EC of the European Parliament and of the Council of 29 April 2004. [Online]. [Accessed 1 June 2018]. Available from: https://eur-lex.europa.eu/LexUriServ/LexUriServ.do?uri=OJ:L:2004:158:0077:0123:en:PDFhttps://eur-lex.europa.eu/LexUriServ/LexUriServ.do?uri=OJ:L:2004:158:0077:0123:en:PDF

EU Council Regulation 2003/2201/EC of 27 November 2003 concerning jurisdiction and the recognition and enforcement of judgments in matrimonial matters and the matters of parental responsibility, repealing Regulation (EC) No 1347/2000. [Online]. [Accessed 25 May 2018]. Available from: http://eur-lex.europa.eu/LexUriServ/LexUriServ.do?uri=CELEX:32003R2201:EN:HTML

EU Council Framework Decision 2002/584/JHA of 13 June 2002 on the European arrest warrant and the surrender procedures between Member States – Statements made by certain Member States on the adoption of the Framework Decision. [Online]. [Accessed 1 June 2018]. Available from: https://eur-lex.europa.eu/legal-content/EN/ALL/?uri=CELEX:32002F0584

EU Parliament and Council Regulation 2016/679/EU of 27 April 2016 on the protection of natural persons with regard to the processing of personal data and on the free movement of such data, and repealing Directive 95/46/EC (General Data Protection Regulation) (text with EEA relevance). [Online]. [Accessed 1 June 2018]. Available from: https://eur-lex.europa.eu/legal-content/EN/TXT/?uri=uriserv:OJ.L_.2016.119.01.0001.01.ENG

European Arrest Warrant Act 2003 (Ireland).

European Commission. (no date[a]) Veterinary border control. [Online]. [Accessed 25 May 2018]. Available from: https://ec.europa.eu/food/animals/vet-border-control_en

European Commission. (no date[b]) Recognition of non-EU financial frameworks (equivalence decisions). [Online]. [Accessed 25 May 2018]. Available from: https://ec.europa.eu/info/business-economy-euro/banking-and-finance/international-relations/recognition-non-eu-financial-frameworks-equivalence-decisions_en

European Commission. (2016) General information about the Customs Union [Online]. [Accessed 24 May 2018]. Available from: http://ec.europa.eu/taxation_customs/40customs/customs_general_info/about/index_en.htm

European Commission. (2018a) Slides on regulatory issues. [Online]. [Accessed 25 May 2018]. Available from: https://ec.europa.eu/commission/publications/slides-regulatory-issues_en

European Commission. (2018b) Negotiating directives for Article 50 negotiations. [Online]. [Accessed 25 May 2018]. Available from: https://ec.europa.eu/commission/publications/negotiating-directives-article-50-negotiations_en

European Communities Act 1972 (UK) (c.68). London: HMSO.

European Convention on Extradition (1957) 359 UNTS 273.

European Convention on Human Rights (1950) 213 UNTS 221.

European Council (2018) Guidelines on the framework for the future EU–UK relationship. [Online]. [Accessed 25 May 2018]. Available from: http://www.consilium.europa.eu/en/press/press-releases/2018/03/23/european-council-art-50-guidelines-on-the-framework-for-the-future-eu-uk-relationship-23-march-2018/

European Parliament (2018) The European Parliament: electoral procedures. [Online]. [Accessed 25 May 2018]. Available from: http://www.europarl.europa.eu/atyourservice/en/displayFtu.html?ftuId=FTU_1.3.4.html

European Parliament Elections Act 1997(Ireland)

European Parliament Elections Act 2013 (Ireland)

European Union (Withdrawal) Act 2018 (UK). London: HMSO.

EU Task Force (European Commission Task Force for the Preparation and Conduct of the Negotiations with the United Kingdom under Article 50 TEU). (2018a) Draft Agreement on the withdrawal of the United Kingdom of Great Britain and Northern Ireland from the European Union and the European Atomic Energy Community, including Protocol on Ireland/Northern Ireland. [Online]. [Accessed 25 May 2018]. Available from: https://ec.europa.eu/commission/sites/beta-political/files/draft_agreement_coloured.pdf

EU Task Force. (2018b) Internal EU27 preparatory discussions for the future relationship: 'regulatory issues'. [Online]. [Accessed 25 May 2018]. Available from: https://ec.europa.eu/commission/sites/beta-political/files/slides_regulatory_issues.pdf

EU Task Force. (2018c) Slides on UK technical note on temporary customs arrangements. [Online] [Accessed 28 June 2018]. Available from: https://ec.europa.eu/commission/sites/beta-political/ files/slides_on_uk_technical_note_on_temporary_customs_ arrangements.pdf

Extradition Act 2003 (UK). (c.41). London: HMSO.

Fenton, S. (2018) *The Good Friday Agreement.* London: Biteback.

Fifth Amendment of the Constitution Act 1972 (Ireland).

Flanagan, C. (2015) *Commencement Matters: International Agreements.* Dublin: Seanad.

Forde, M. and Leonard, D. (2013) *Constitutional Law of Ireland.* London: A&C Black.

Foster, A. (2016) Interview: The Marr Show, BBC1. [Online]. 15 May, Tyrone. [Accessed 28 May 2018]. Available from: https:// www.bbc.co.uk/programmes/p03v6bhc

Foster, R. (2007) *Luck and the Irish: A Brief History of Change 1970–2000.* London: Allen Lane.

FSVO (Federal Food Safety and Veterinary Office). (2017) Veterinary agreement between Switzerland and the EU. [Online]. [Accessed 25 May 2018]. Available from: https://www.blv.admin.ch/blv/ en/home/das-blv/kooperationen/internationale-abkommen/ veterinaerabkommen-schweiz-eu.html#context-sidebar

Gallagher v Lynn [1937] AC 863.

Godson, D. (2005) *Himself Alone: David Trimble and the Ordeal of Unionism.* London: HarperCollins UK.

Good, J. (1922) Partition in practice. *Studies: An Irish Quarterly Review* 11: 265.

Gordon, M. (2016) The UK's sovereignty situation: Brexit, bewilderment and beyond…. *King's Law Journal* 27: 333.

Government of Ireland Act 1920 (UK) (10&11 Geo.5, c.67). London: HMSO.

Griffith, J.A.G. (1979) The political constitution. *Modern Law Review* 42(1): 1.

Grimson, A. (2018) The Brexit negotiation – Dodds warns against the 'annexation' of Northern Ireland. *ConservativeHome*. [Online]. [Accessed 28 May 2018]. Available from: https://www.conservativehome.com/highlights/2018/04/interview-the-brexit-negotiation-dodds-warns-against-the-annexation-of-northern-ireland.html

Hainsworth, P. (1981) Northern Ireland: a European role? *Journal of Common Market Studies* 20(1): 1–15.

Halleskov, L. (2005) The Long-Term Residents Directive: a fulfilment of the Tampere objective of near-equality. *European Journal of Migration and Law* 7(2): 181.

Harvey, C. (2001) Building bridges – protecting human rights in Northern Ireland. *Hum. Rts. L. Rev.* 1: 243.

Hayward, K. (2017) The origins of the Irish border. [Online]. [Accessed 25 May 2018]. Available from: http://ukandeu.ac.uk/explainers/the-origins-of-the-irish-border/

Heaney, S. (2002) Through-other places, through-other times: the Irish poet and Britain. In: *Finders Keepers: Selected Prose 1971–2001*. New York, NY: Farrar, Straus and Giroux, p. 396.

Helm, T. and Savage, M. (2018) Brexit realists take control as May slaps down Rees-Mogg. *The Observer*. [Online]. 20 May. [Accessed 28 May 2018]. Available from: https://www.theguardian.com/politics/2018/may/20/theresa-may-brexit-realists-jacob-rees-mogg

Hermon, S. *Hansard* HC Deb. vol.631, col.941, 21 Nov 2017.

Hewitt, J. (1964) Extract from a letter to John Montague. John Hewitt Collection, University of Ulster.

HM Treasury (2017) *Customs Bill: Legislating for the UK's Future Customs, VAT and Excise Regimes*. (Cm 9502). London: HMSO.

HM Treasury, HM Revenue and Customs and Department for Exiting the European Union. (2017) Future customs arrangements – a future partnership paper. [Online]. [Accessed 25 May 2018]. Available from: https://assets.publishing.service.gov.uk/government/uploads/system/uploads/attachment_data/file/637748/Future_customs_arrangements_-_a_future_partnership_paper.pdf

Home Office. (2017a) Current account closed or refused based on immigration status. [Online]. [Accessed 11 January 2018]. Available from: https://www.gov.uk/government/publications/current-account-closed-or-refused-based-on-immigration-status

Home Office. (2017b) Home Office immigration & nationality charges. [Online]. [Accessed 10 January 2018]. Available from: https://www.gov.uk/government/uploads/system/uploads/attachment_data/file/607212/Fees_table_April_2017.pdf

Horgan, J. (1939) Ulster, Ireland, Britain. *International Affairs* 18: 425.

House of Commons Business, Energy and Industrial Strategy Committee. (2017) *Oral Evidence: Leaving the EU: Implications for the Automotive Industry*. (HC 379). London: HMSO.

House of Commons European Scrutiny Committee. (2013) *The UK's Block Opt-Out of Pre-Lisbon Criminal Law and Policing Measures*. (HC 683). London: HMSO.

House of Commons European Scrutiny Committee. (2018) *EU Withdrawal: Transitional Provisions and Dispute Resolution*. (HC 763). London: HMSO.

House of Commons Exiting the European Union Committee. (2018a) *The Progress of the UK's Negotiations on EU Withdrawal: December 2017 to March 2018*. (HC 884). London: HMSO.

House of Commons Exiting the European Union Committee. (2018b) *The Future UK–EU Relationship.* (HC 935). London: HMSO.

House of Lords European Union Committee. (2016a) *Brexit: Future UK–EU Security and Police Cooperation*. (HL 77). London: HMSO.

House of Lords European Union Committee. (2016b) *Brexit: UK–Irish Relations.* (HL 76). London: HMSO.

Houses of the Oireachtas. (2018) Taoiseach's meetings and engagements 08/05/2018. [Online]. [Accessed 25 May 2018]. Available from: https://www.oireachtas.ie/en/debates/question/2018-05-08/10/

Human Rights Act 1998 (UK). (c.42). London: HMSO.

Human Rights Consortium. (2018) *Rights at Risk: Brexit, Human Rights and Northern Ireland*. [Online]. [Accessed 25 May 2018]. Available from: http://www.humanrightsconsortium.org/wp-content/uploads/2018/01/RIGHTS-AT-RISK-Final.pdf

Human Rights Council. (2014) Report of the Special Rapporteur on adequate housing as a component of the right to an adequate standard of living, and on the right to non-discrimination in this context. *United Nations General Assembly*, A/HRC/25/54/Add.2. [Online]. [Accessed 25 May 2018]. Available from: http://www.ohchr.org/EN/HRBodies/HRC/RegularSessions/Session25/Pages/ListReports.aspx

Imana, S. (2009) *Rules of Origin in International Trade.* Cambridge: Cambridge University Press.

Immigration Act 1971 (UK). (c.77). London: HMSO.

Informal Committee on the Constitution. (1967) Report of the Committee on the Constitution. Dublin.

In re Logue [1933] 67 ILTR 253.

In re Parsons Application for Judicial Review [2003] NICA 20.

Institute for Government. (2017) Trade after Brexit: options for the UK's relationship with the EU. [Online]. [Accessed 25 May 2018]. Available from: https://www.instituteforgovernment.org.uk/sites/default/files/publications/IFGJ5896-Brexit-Report-171214-final_0.pdf

Intermediate Education (Ireland) Act 1878 (UK). (c.66) London: HMSO.

International Court of Justice. (2018) Declarations recognizing the jurisdiction of the Court as compulsory. [Online]. [Accessed 25 May 2018]. Available from: http://www.icj-cij.org/en/declarations

International Law Commission. (2001) *Draft Articles on Responsibility of States for Internationally Wrongful Acts, With Commentaries*. GA Resolution A/56/10.

Ireland Act 1949 (UK) (14 Geo.6, c.41). London: HMSO.

Irish Free State (Special Duties) Act 1932 (UK). (c.30) London: HMSO.

Irish Nationality and Citizenship Act 1956 (Ireland). (No. 26 of 1956).

Joint Committee on European Union Affairs. (2014) *Voting Rights of Irish Citizens Abroad*. 31ENUA0018.

Joint Declaration on Peace: The Downing Street Declaration, 15 December 1993.

Joint Report (2017) Joint Report from the Negotiators of the European Union and the United Kingdom government on progress during phase 1 of negotiations under Article 50 TEU on the United Kingdom's orderly withdrawal from the EU. [Online]. [Accessed 25 May 2018]. Available from: https://ec.europa.eu/commission/sites/beta-political/files/joint_report.pdf

Jones, D. *Hansard* HC Deb. vol.620, col.1170, 1 February 2017.

Kearney, R. (2010) Renarrating Irish politics in a European context. *European Studies* 28: 41.

King, A. (2009) *The British Constitution*. Oxford: Oxford University Press.

King v Attorney General [1981] IR 233.

Leary, P. (2016) *Unapproved Routes: Histories of the Irish Border 1922–1972*. Oxford: Oxford University Press.

Lee, P. *Hansard HC Written Question*. 7772, 12 September 2017.

Liddington, D. (2018) United at home, stronger abroad. [Online]. 26 February, Broughton. [Accessed 25 May 2018]. Available from: https://www.gov.uk/government/speeches/united-at-home-stronger-abroad

Logan, E. (2018) Belfast (Good Friday) Agreement Joint Committee warns of Brexit human rights and equality concerns. [Online]. [Accessed 25 May 2018]. Available from: https://www.ihrec.ie/belfast-good-friday-agreement-joint-committee-warns-brexit-human-rights-equality-concerns/

Lowe, S. (2016) Explaining cumulative rules of origin. *Medium*. [Online]. 25 November. [Accessed 25 May 2018]. Available from: https://medium.com/@SamuelMarcLowe/explaining-cumulative-rules-of-origin-2c13fb4dfca1

Maciejewski, M. and Dancourt, L. (2017) The internal market: general principles. [Online]. [Accessed 25 May 2018]. Available from: http://www.europarl.europa.eu/aboutparliament/en/displayFtu.html?ftuId=FTU_2.1.1.html

Mallie, E. and McKittrick, D. (1997) *The Fight for Peace: Secret Story Behind the Irish Peace Process*. London: Mandarin.

Martin v Lord Advocate [2010] UKSC 10

May, T. (2014a) *Hansard* HC Deb, vol. 587, col. 1229, 10 November 2014.

May, T. (2014b) *Hansard* HC Deb, vol. 584, col. 491, 10 July 2014.

May, T. (2016) Home Secretary's speech on the UK, EU and our place in the world. [Online]. 25 April, London. [Accessed 31 May 2018]. Available from: https://www.gov.uk/government/speeches/home-secretarys-speech-on-the-uk-eu-and-our-place-in-the-world

May, T. (2017a) *The United Kingdom's exit from and new partnership with the European Union* (Cm.9417). [Online]. [Accessed 25 May 2018]. Available from: https://assets.publishing.service. gov.uk/government/uploads/system/uploads/attachment_data/ file/589191/The_United_Kingdoms_exit_from_and_partnership_ with_the_EU_Web.pdf

May, T. (2017b) *Hansard* HC Deb, vol. 624, col. 251-252, 29 March 2017.

May, T. (2017c) The government's negotiating objectives for exiting the EU: PM speech. [Online]. 17 January. [Accessed 25 May 2018]. Available from: https://www.gov.uk/government/speeches/the-governments-negotiating-objectives-for-exiting-the-eu-pm-speech

May, T. (2017d) PM's Florence speech: a new era of cooperation and partnership between the UK and the EU. [Online]. 22 September, Florence. [Accessed 25 May 2018]. Available from: https://www. gov.uk/government/speeches/pms-florence-speech-a-new-era-of-cooperation-and-partnership-between-the-uk-and-the-eu

May, T. (2018a) Trust me, I'll take back control – but I'll need your help. *Sunday Times*. 13 May.

May, T. (2018b) PM speech on our future economic partnership with the European Union. [Online]. 2 March, London. [Accessed 25 May 2018]. Available from: https://www.gov.uk/government/ speeches/pm-speech-on-our-future-economic-partnership-with-the-european-union

May, T. (2018c) PM speech at Munich Security Conference. [Online]. 17 February, Munich. [Accessed 25 May 2018]. Available from: https://www.gov.uk/government/speeches/pm-speech-at-munich-security-conference-17-february-2018 McCrudden, C. and Halberstam, D. (2017) Miller and Northern Ireland: a critical constitutional response. *UK Supreme Court Yearbook* 8: 299.

May, T. (2018d) *The future relationship between the United Kingdom and the European Union* (Cm.9593). [Online]. [Accessed 16 July 2018]. Available from: https://assets.publishing.service.gov.uk/government/uploads/system/uploads/attachment_data/file/725288/The_future_relationship_between_the_United_Kingdom_and_the_European_Union.pdf

McCrudden, C., Ford, R. and Heath, A. (2004) Legal regulation of affirmative action in Northern Ireland: an empirical assessment. *Oxford Journal of Legal Studies* 24: 363.

McDonald, H. (2018) David Trimble: Ireland risks provoking paramilitaries over post-Brexit border. *The Guardian*. [Online]. 6 April. [Accessed 25 May 2018]. Available from: https://www.theguardian.com/world/2018/apr/06/david-trimble-ireland-risks-provoking-paramilitaries-over-post-brexit-border

McGee v Attorney General [1974] IR 284.

McGimpsey v Ireland [1990] IR 110.

Meehan, E. (2000) 'Britain's Irish question: Britain's European question?' British–Irish relations in the context of European Union and The Belfast Agreement. *Review of International Studies* 26(1): 83.

Milk and Milk Products Act (NI) 1934 (UK).

Milne, A. A. (1926) *Winnie-the-Pooh*. London: Methuen & Co.

Minister for Justice and Equality v O'Connor [2018] IESC 3.

Mitsilegas, V. (2016) The uneasy relationship between the UK and European criminal law: from optouts to Brexit? *Criminal Law Review* 517.

Morgan, A. (2001) What Bill of Rights? *Northern Ireland Legal Quarterly* 52: 234.

Morgan, A. (2011) *The Hand of History: Legal Essays on the Belfast Agreement*. London.

Morrison, J. and Livingstone, S. (1995) *Reshaping Public Power: Northern Ireland and the British Constitutional Crisis*. London: Sweet & Maxwell.

Murphy, M. (2016) *Northern Ireland and the European Union: The Dynamics of a Changing Relationship*. Oxford: Oxford University Press.

Newark, F.H. (1954) Judicial review of confiscatory legislation under the Northern Ireland Constitution. *American Journal of Comparative Law* 3: 552.

NIAC (House of Commons Northern Ireland Affairs Committee). (2016) *Oral Evidence: Future of the Land Border with the Republic of Ireland*. (HC 700). London: The HMSO.

NIAC. (2018a) *The Land Border between Northern Ireland and Ireland*. (HC 329). London: HMSO.

NIAC. (2018b) *Oral Evidence: Devolution and Democracy in Northern Ireland – Dealing with the Deficit*. (HC 613). London: HMSO.

Norris v Attorney General [1984] IR 36.

Northern Ireland Act 1998 (UK) (c.47). London: HMSO.

Northern Ireland Assembly Standing Orders (2016). [Online]. [Accessed 25 May 2018]. Available from: http://www.niassembly.gov.uk/globalassets/documents/standing-orders/so-oct-2016updates.pdf

Northern Ireland Executive. (2015) A fresh start: the Stormont Agreement and implementation plan. [Online]. November. [Accessed 25 May 2018]. Available from: https://assets.publishing.service.gov.uk/government/uploads/system/uploads/attachment_data/file/479116/A_Fresh_Start_-_The_Stormont_Agreement_and_Implementation_Plan_-_Final_Version_20_Nov_2015_for_PDF.pdf

Northern Ireland Government. (1956) *Why the Border Must Be: The Northern Ireland Case in Brief*. London: HMSO.

Northern Ireland Human Rights Commission. (2018) Out of sight, out of mind: Traveller's accommodation in Northern Ireland. [Online]. [Accessed 25 May 2018]. Available from: http://www.nihrc.org/publication/detail/out-of-sight-out-of-mind-travellers-accommodation-in-ni-full-report

Northern Ireland Statistics and Research Agency. (2012) *Census 2011: key statistics for Northern Ireland.* [Online]. [Accessed 25 May 2018]. Available from: https://www.nisra.gov.uk/sites/nisra.gov.uk/files/publications/2011-census-results-key-statistics-northern-ireland-report-11-december-2012.pdf

O'Brien, C., Spaventa, E. and De Connick, J. (2016) Comparative report: the concept of worker under Article 45 TFEU and certain non-standard forms of employment. [Online]. [Accessed 26 May 2018]. Available from: ec.europa.eu/social/BlobServlet?docId=1 5476&langId=en

Ó Caoindealbháin, B. (2006) Citizenship and borders: Irish Nationality law and Northern Ireland. Mapping Frontiers. Plotting Pathways Working Paper No. 18.

O'Duffy, B. (1999) British and Irish conflict regulation from Sunningdale to Belfast Part I: tracing the status of contesting sovereigns, 1968–1974. *Nations and Nationalism* 5: 523.

Office of the Deputy Prime Minister. (2001) *Memorandum of Understanding and Supplementary Agreements between the UK Government and the Devolved Administrations.* (Cm.5240). London: HMSO.

Ostrom, E. (1990) *Governing the Commons: The Evolution of Institutions for Collective Action.* Cambridge: Cambridge University Press.

Paisley, I. *Hansard* HC Deb. vol.632, col. 1105, 06 December 2017.

Parker, G. (2018) Time for UK to make a choice on Brexit trade future, warns Barnier. *Financial Times.* [Online]. 5 February. [Accessed 25 May 2018]. Available from: https://www.ft.com/content/95daa612-0a74-11e8-839d-41ca06376bf2

Parliamentary Papers of Northern Ireland (1922) *Volume 2.*

Patten, C. *Hansard* HL Deb. vol.790, col.286, 21 March 2018.

Patterson, H. (1999) Sean Lemass and the Ulster question, 1959–65. *Journal of Contemporary History* 34: 145.

Peyton, J. *Hansard* HC Deb. vol.888 col.433, 11 March 1975.

Peyton, M. (2016) Ian Paisley Jr urges Northern Irish citizens to apply for Republic of Ireland passports. *The Independent*. [Online]. 25 June. [Accessed 25 May 2018]. Available from: https://www. independent.co.uk/news/uk/politics/unionist-ian-paisley-jr-mp-constituents-apply-republic-of-ireland-eire-passports-a7102761. html

Police (Northern Ireland) Act 2000. (c.32). London: HMSO.

PricewaterhouseCoopers. (2001) North/South Ministerial Council: study of obstacles to mobility. [Online]. [Accessed 26 May 2018]. Available from: http://www.espaces-transfrontaliers.org/fileadmin/user_upload/documents/Documents_Fiches_Projets/obstacles-to-cross-border-mobility_border_people.pdf

Protocol on the Concerns of the Irish People on the Treaty of Lisbon (2013) Official Journal of the European Union L 60/131.

PSNI (Police Service of Northern Ireland). (2018) Trends in hate motivated incidents and crimes recorded by the police in Northern Ireland 2004/05 to 2016/17. [Online]. [Accessed 10 January 2018]. Available from: https://www.psni.police.uk/globalassets/inside-the-psni/our-statistics/hate-motivation-statistics/hate-motivated-incidents-and-crimes-in-northern-ireland-2004-05-to-2016-17. pdf

Question Time – Declan Kearney. (2016) BBC1. 21 January. [Online]. [Accessed 28 May 2018]. Available from: https://www.bbc.co.uk/programmes/b06yms21

Raab, D. *Hansard* HC Deb. vol.633, col.489, 13 December 2017.

Re Criminal Law (Jurisdiction) Bill 1975 1 IR 129

Ritchie, M. *Hansard* HC Deb. vol.620, cols.973-974, 31 January 2017.

R (Miller) v Secretary of State for Exiting the European Union [2017] UKSC 5.

Robinson v Secretary of State for Northern Ireland [2002] UKHL 32.

Rogers, S. (2016) Irish passport applications surge by almost 50,000. *The Irish Examiner*. [Online]. 10 August. [Accessed 28 May 2018]. Available from: https://www.irishexaminer.com/ireland/irish-passport-applications-surge-by-almost-50000-415066.html

Royce, M. (2017) *The Political Theology of European Integration: Comparing the Influence of Religious Histories on European Policies.* London: Palgrave Macmillan.

Rudd, A. (2017) *The United Kingdom's Exit from the European Union: Safeguarding the Position of EU Citizens Living in the UK and UK Nationals Living in the EU.* (Cm.9464). [Online]. London: HMSO. [Accessed 26 May 2018]. Available from: https://www.gov.uk/government/publications/safeguarding-the-position-of-eu-citizens-in-the-uk-and-uk-nationals-in-the-eu/the-united-kingdoms-exit-from-the-european-union-safeguarding-the-position-of-eu-citizens-living-in-the-uk-and-uk-nationals-living-in-the-eu

R v Secretary of State for the Home Department, ex parte Simms [1999] 3 All ER 400.

R v Secretary of State for Transport, ex parte Factortame (No. 2) [1991] 1 AC 603.

Ryan, B. (2001) The Common Travel Area between Britain and Ireland. *Modern Law Review* 64: 855.

Ryan, B. (2004) The Celtic cubs: the controversy over birthright citizenship in Ireland. *European Journal of Migration and Law* 6: 173.

Sales, R. (1997) *Women Divided: Gender, Religion and Politics in Northern Ireland.* London: Routledge.

Schweitzer, D.R. (1984) The failure of William Pitt's Irish trade propositions 1785. *Parliamentary History* 3: 129.

Scotch Whisky Association v Lord Advocate [2017] UKSC 76.

Scotland Act 1998 (UK) (c.46). London: HMSO.

Sewel, B., *Hansard*, HL Deb, vol. 592, col. 791, 21 July 1998.

Sex Discrimination (Northern Ireland) Order 1976 (UK). London: HMSO.

Slobodian, Q. (2018) *Globalists: The End of Empire and the Birth of Neoliberalism.* Cambridge: Harvard University Press.

Smith, A. (2018) The EU should agree an all-UK backstop. [Online]. [Accessed 25 May 2018]. Available from: https://blogs.sussex.ac.uk/uktpo/2018/05/22/the-eu-should-agree-an-all-uk-backstop/

Smith, A., McWilliams, M. and Yarnell, P. (2016) Does every cloud have a silver lining: Brexit, repeal of the Human Rights Act and the Northern Ireland Bill of Rights. *Fordham International Law Journal* 40: 79.

Smith, E. (2016) Policing the Northern Irish border in the 1970s. [Online]. [Accessed 24 May 2018]. Available from: https://hatfulofhistory.wordpress.com/2016/06/17/policing-the-northern-irish-border-in-the-1970s/

Sparrow, A. (2018) EU has 'pushed back' on UK customs proposals, Davis tells Lords – as it happened. *The Guardian*. [Online]. 1 May. [Accessed 24 May 2018]. Available from: https://www.theguardian.com/politics/blog/live/2018/may/01/brexit-david-davis-lords-liam-fox-tells-may-that-compromising-over-customs-union-would-be-unacceptable-politics-live?page=with:block-5ae89294e4b0f016ba584c4e#block-5ae89294e4b0f016ba584c4e

Taylor, A.J.P. (1971) *Lloyd George: Twelve Essays*. London: Hamish Hamilton.

The State (Healy) v Donoghue [1976] IR 325.

Third Amendment of the Constitution Act 1972 (Ireland).

Thoburn v Sunderland City Council [2002] EWHC 195.

Trade Bill 2017–19 (UK). London: HMSO.

Trauner, F. (2016) Asylum policy: the EU's 'crises' and the looming policy regime failure. *Journal of European Integration* 38: 311.

Treaty Establishing the European Economic Community (1957) 298 UNTS 11.

Treaty on European Union [1992] OJ C326.

Treaty on European Union (Consolidated version) (2016) OJ C 202

Treaty on the Functioning of the European Union (Consolidated version) (2016) OJ C 202

Trimble, D. (2017) The Taoiseach should stop trying to out-Sinn Fein Sinn Fein. *The Spectator*. [Online]. 29 November. [Accessed 31 May 2018]. Available from: https://blogs.spectator.co.uk/2017/11/david-trimble-the-taoiseach-should-stop-trying-to-out-sinn-fein-sinn-fein/

TUC (Trade Unions Congress) (2016) Employment rights and the EU. [Online]. [Accessed 25 May 2018]. Available from: https://www.tuc.org.uk/sites/default/files/UK%20employment%20rights%20and%20the%20EU.pdf

UK–EU Joint Technical Note. (2017) Joint technical notes on citizen's rights. [Online]. December. [Accessed 26 May 2018]. Available from: https://assets.publishing.service.gov.uk/government/uploads/system/uploads/attachment_data/file/665871/December_-_Joint_technical_note_on_the_comparison_of_EU-UK_positions_on_citizens__rights.pdf

UK Government. (no date) Pay for UK healthcare as part of your immigration application: how much you have to pay. [Online]. [Accessed 11 January 2018]. Available from: https://www.gov.uk/healthcare-immigration-application/how-much-pay

UK Government. (2017a) Northern Ireland and Ireland (position paper). [Online]. [Accessed 25 May 2018]. Available from: https://assets.publishing.service.gov.uk/government/uploads/system/uploads/attachment_data/file/638135/6.3703_DEXEU_Northern_Ireland_and_Ireland_INTERACTIVE.pdf

UK Government. (2017b) Status of EU citizens in the UK: what you need to know. [Online]. [Accessed 25 May 2018]. Available from: https://www.gov.uk/guidance/status-of-eu-nationals-in-the-uk-what-you-need-to-know

UK Government. (2017c) Technical note: citizen's rights, administrative procedures in the UK. [Online]. [Accessed 26 May 2018]. Available from: https://www.gov.uk/government/publications/citizens-rights-administrative-procedures-in-the-uk/technical-note-citizens-rights-administrative-procedures-in-the-uk

Vienna Convention on the Law of Treaties (1969) 1155 UNTS 331.

Villiers, T. *Westminster Hall*, col.197WH, 16 Jul 2013.

Wade, H.W.R. (1955) The legal basis of sovereignty. *Common Law Journal* 172.

Wade, H.W.R. (1996) Sovereignty – revolution or evolution? *Law Quarterly Review* 112: 568.

Walker, R. *Hansard* HC Deb, vol. 632, col. 1093, 6 December 2017.

Weatherill, S. (2014) Why there is no 'principle of mutual recognition' in EU law (and why that matters to consumer lawyers). In: Purnhagen, K. and Roth, P. (eds) *Varieties of European Economic Law and Regulation*. New York, NY: Springer.

Weiler, J. (1990) The European Community in change: exit, voice and loyalty. *Irish Studies in International Affairs* 3: 15.

Weyembergh, A. (2017) Consequences of Brexit for European Union criminal law. New Journal of European Criminal Law 8: 284.

Wills, J. and Warwick, B.T.C. (2016) Contesting austerity: the potential and pitfalls of socioeconomic rights discourse. *Indiana Journal of Global Legal Studies* 23(2).

World Customs Organisation (2012) Accumulation/cumulation. [Online]. [Accessed 25 May 2018]. Available from: http://www.wcoomd.org/en/topics/origin/instrument-and-tools/comparative-study-on-preferential-rules-of-origin/specific-topics/study-topics/cum.aspx

Wright, O., Waterfield, B., Elliott, F. and Coates, S. (2018) May seeks new Brexit transition to 2023. *The Times*. [Online]. 24 May. [Accessed 25 May 2018]. Available from: https://www.thetimes.co.uk/edition/news/may-seeks-new-brexit-transition-to-2023-qj86h3fhv

Index

Note: Page numbers for tables appear in italics.